Simple Cooperation in the Classroom

Jacqueline Rhoades

and

Margaret E. McCabe

ITA Publications, Willits, California

Simple Cooperation in the Classroom

Published by:

ITA Publications
P.O. Box 1599
Willits, CA 95490-1599, U.S.A.

Library of Congress Catalog Card Number: 85-80102

ISBN 0-933935-07-2   soft cover

To our grandchildren **Jenna** and Mellissa.

CONTENTS

CHARTS AND ILLUSTRATIONS

ACKNOWLEDGEMENTS

A special THANK YOU to Neva Beach for her fine job of editing and to Carolyn Brown for her excellent job of proofing. We also want to thank our workshop participants who have contributed to our ideas and so strongly encouraged us to write this book.

A special thanks to Judith Hummer, Marvin Roupe, Dr. Stan Schainker, and Ann Marie Samson for contributing to the activities section; to Letitia Solomon for allowing us to include her book as the basis for an activity; and to Diana Nickerman for drawing the characatures.

Finally, our appreciation goes to Dr. S. Norman Feingold for taking time from his own hectic schedule to read our manuscript and write the foreword.

FOREWORD

When I was invited to write the Foreword for *Simple Cooperation in The Classroom,* in spite of pressing deadlines there was no hesitation on my part. The high regard I have for the two professional colleagues who have authored this book will be obvious. Moreover, I am biased since I am a futurist who is an optimist by conviction and temperament.

Simple Cooperation in The Classroom is written in an easy-to-read style by two prominent educators. The book is chock-full of practical guidelines and suggestions garnered from their 25 years of teaching and administrative experience in the United State and other countries. Teaching of academic and social skills under one umbrella is highlighted. Forms, charts, and figures as well as lesson designs and plans are clearly presented and are easy to follow and to put into practice. Each chapter has a succinct overview of its contents. One chapter logically blends into the next one.

Section 2 lists creative activities by grade and time line as a resource and a plan to begin educational growth and development. Social and thinking skills in coping, and skills needed in earning a livelihood are top priority. Students in elementary school today will probably have at least six different careers during their work lives. Many will probably be working until 2075. The 21st Century is almost here.

The authors provide many opportunities and challenges to make a big educational difference. Students need to grow throughout their life span or they will become as obsolete as a machine. The authors underline the need for students to have good communication skills not only in reading and writing but also in speaking and listening as well. *Simple Cooperation in The Classroom* offers challenging effective education techniques so that teachers and their students need not become obsolete.

Accountability and changing challenges which have been greater for educators will remain priorities to the year 2000 and beyond. The authors understand the educational process. Theory is not minimized but the book's thrust and philosophy is to provide practical skills and resources to meet the varying needs and aspirations of educators and their students. This book emphasizes the resolution of educational problems.

Hundreds of books are written each year on the subject of teaching and education. *Simple Cooperation in The Classroom* by Jacqueline Rhoades and Margaret E. McCabe is in the vanguard of the list of books that not only must be read but must also be used to make a significant difference in the lives of students and teachers.

The authors ask for feedback from users in order to improve future revisions. *Simple Cooperation in The Classroom* is a user friendly book and is a rich resource of information and techniques that work. It should be on every teacher's desk for bottom line efficiency. Don't leave for school without it.

S. Norman Feingold, Ed.D.
President, National Career
and Counseling Services
Washington, D.C. 20005

NOTES FROM PEGGY AND JACQUIE

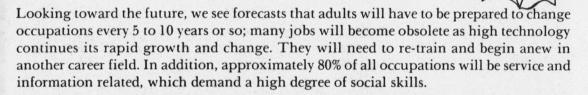

We welcome you to Simple Cooperation!

Simple Cooperation is designed to prepare our students for the future. A future that demands life-long growth and the ability to adjust.

During this last decade educators have been concerned, for we see many of our students graduating from school without the necessary skills to succeed in the work world. In many instances students have few, if any, marketable skills. In addition, after obtaining employment, many lose their jobs because they are unable to communicate clearly and "get along" with other people.

Looking toward the future, we see forecasts that adults will have to be prepared to change occupations every 5 to 10 years or so; many jobs will become obsolete as high technology continues its rapid growth and change. They will need to re-train and begin anew in another career field. In addition, approximately 80% of all occupations will be service and information related, which demand a high degree of social skills.

If we, as teachers, examine the present state of "educational affairs" and seriously look at the forecasts of what will be required of our future graduates, we must each ask "What can I do to prepare my students for the world to come?" Using Simple Cooperation in your classroom is one place to begin, for it combines the teaching of ACADEMIC and SOCIAL SKILLS under one instructional umbrella. One of its many strong points is that Simple Cooperation may be used at any grade level (pre-school through adult) and with any subject matter. You need only to adjust the process and content to fit the students that you are teaching.

The Simple Cooperation model has evolved over a period of time — many years, in fact. It has emerged from our own growth process as teachers grappling with the same issues that every teacher seems to deal with on a day to day basis: not enough time, discipline problems, curriculum requirements, and on, and on. It's a tough job to be a teacher. In the future our job will be even more challenging! It is our belief that using Simple Cooperation in your classroom will make that job just a little bit easier, and the job of learning easier for your students.

The concept of cooperative learning began a long time ago. It finds its "formal" origin in the works of pioneer sociologists and psychologists. More importantly, perhaps, is the recognition that it found its "informal" beginning in thousands, if not millions, of individual classrooms all over the world throughout the history of education. The idea of cooperative groups is not new: teachers have been using cooperation for a long time. Teachers really do seem to have an "extra sense" that tells us that kids learn from kids, sometimes even better than they learn from us.

A number of cooperative learning models have been developed in recent years. Sometimes they have been clearly identified as cooperative models. In other instances they have simply been viewed by their creators as methods of accomplishing objectives by having kids work together toward a common goal. In the reference section we have listed a number of books which we encourage you to review. They will expand upon the concepts presented in the Simple Cooperation model and enlarge your lesson plan repertoire.

We recognize that even thinking about changing your instructional format could cause sweat to come to your brow and a huge lump to form in your throat. Change does not come easy. To you, with these feelings, we say — HANG ON — its not as tough as first glance would indicate. In the beginning you will have to work a little harder; however, after you've implemented Simple Cooperation in your classroom and have gained some experience with the process, it will make your job a lot easier.

Move at your own pace. Take time to master each step before moving on. No doubt your anxiety will soon be replaced with a broad smile because, if your experience is like ours, your students will learn more in a shorter period of time; they will also have fewer problems interacting with each other (in and out of the classroom). To make a long story short, your job will no doubt be easier and you will most likely feel better about what you are doing.

It is important to realize that while you are feeling the pangs of uncertainty about changing your style, your students may also have these feelings (though in all probability they will adapt and enjoy more quickly than adults). At any rate, this is another reason we suggest that you move slowly. Both you and your students need time to become accustomed to the change of style. Begin small, learn it well, then take another step. A systematic approach to infusing Simple Cooperation into your curriculum will benefit both you and your students.

It is also important to recognize that the first few times you initiate a Simple Cooperation lesson, it may not be a raging success. OR perhaps all will go well the first several lessons, then without warning your cooperative lesson falls apart. DO NOT GIVE UP! This is a phenomenon that happens. Sometimes we can determine what went wrong, sometimes we can't. The important thing is that you attempt to analyze what has happened, revise your process and do it again.

We have a cumulative 25 years experience working with groups and every once in a while we 'bomb' — maybe we were off target just a little bit, or maybe one of us wasn't feeling terrific, or maybe it was just the composition of the group and we didn't become aware of that particular group's 'personality' fast enough to adjust our approach. It really hurts the ego, but we try to look at it as a learning experience. We truly hope you will do the same thing. SIMPLE COOPERATION DOES WORK — give it, and yourself multiple chances for success.

Please know that, in our opinion, there is only one correct method of implementing Simple Cooperation in your classroom. That is the one that best suits you. We have provided a portrait of Simple Cooperation; it is but our picture frozen in space and time. In reality, Simple Cooperation is a fluid, evolving entity. Each person using the model designs his/her own applications of the concepts presented here.

A genuine attempt has been made to credit the originators of activities and concepts presented in Simple Cooperation in the Classroom. We found that this was not an easy task. Activities have been reproduced in workshops, lectures have been given, and books have been written throughout the years without credit being given to the originator. In addition, activities have been developed by one individual, only to find that someone else has developed the same activity at another place or time. We have, whenever possible, given credit to the originator of each concept and activity included in this book. If we have given credit to someone other than the originator, or have not given credit where credit is due, it is unintentional.

We have attempted to write this book in 'every day' language — nothing fancy. No doubt, we have not avoided all 'educationese' or 'academicese' — we did try, however. Your feedback on the style, content, and your own personal experience with Simple Cooperation is most welcome. Please address any feedback to:

Jacquie and Peggy
ITA Publications
P.O. Box 1599
Willits, CA 95490

We look forward to hearing from you!

CHAPTER 1
WELCOME TO SIMPLE COOPERATION

OVERVIEW
This chapter introduces you to Simple Cooperation and its underlying philosophy. Several aspects of Simple Cooperation are discussed including group development, conflict, problem solving, group roles, and the teacher as facilitator.

If you were to walk into a Simple Cooperation classroom the first thing you might notice is that the students are clustered in small groups at workplaces around the room. As you watched, you would begin to see an unusual level of concentration in the groups, a focus on the work at hand in each one. You might remark on the lack of distracting behavior; if the groups were working orally in a discussion, you would hear students speaking one at a time, to the point of the lesson, without wisecracking or irrelevant remarks. Yet in all this focused concentration, an atmosphere of support and friendliness would pervade the room.

Walking into a Simple Cooperation classroom

The groups of students might be studying spelling, or history, or geography or math — any of the subjects that are usually taught in the classroom, for Simple Cooperation fits easily into any curriculum. And in spite of the unusually high level of relaxed concentration, the students would possess the usual mix of skill levels and emotional development, for Simple Cooperation works with any age and any set of students. It can work for you and your students, too.

WHY BOTHER?

Let's assume that our task as teachers is to prepare our students to perform at their maximum potential — to be prepared for life to the fullest extent of their capabilities.

Our task as teachers

Let's recognize the discrepancy between this assumption and what is actually happening in the educational system today.

It's widely accepted that far too few students are adequately prepared academically. But they suffer from another gap in their education as well: one that is at least as crippling to them. They are even less prepared in the social skills they need — the ability to communicate clearly and function well with other people.

Such social skills are essential in almost every aspect of life. Certainly they're essential in school, and will be crucial in the working world for which we must prepare our students. In the adult world, there are few jobs that involve working alone. Most occupations, even apparently isolated ones such as library or research work, involve some degree of interaction with others. Our students will be required to work with others throughout their lives. Yet the social skills required for good group and interpersonal functioning are rarely taught. It's assumed that students will somehow just pick them up or absorb them from the air. Some do. More do not, or do so only imperfectly.'

Social Skills are essential

Social Skills are rarely taught

Simple Cooperation offers a classroom model that lets you add instruction in these social skills even as it improves learning of regular academic skills.

GETTING A START

Simple Cooperation combines academic study with group development and meeting management techniques which, when combined, form the social skills component (see Figure 1).

Combining academic and social skills

It takes seriously the students' need to learn good communication skills; not just reading and writing, but speaking and listening as well. With this model you will learn simple group techniques and activities to use in making a collection of individuals — your class — into a unified, cooperative group with a shared purpose. You will learn how a group works and how to direct its working to increase the level of academic and social skills of its members.

The Simple Cooperation group development model begins with activities and techniques to establish a secure, supportive environment in the classroom. The first step is the teacher SETTING STANDARDS. Then, students get to know you and each other through GETTING ACQUAINTED activities. Their attention and energies are re-focused at the beginning of each day and after lunch and recess or breaks with simple TRANSITION and ENERGIZING activities.

Figure 1. Major components of Simple Cooperation.

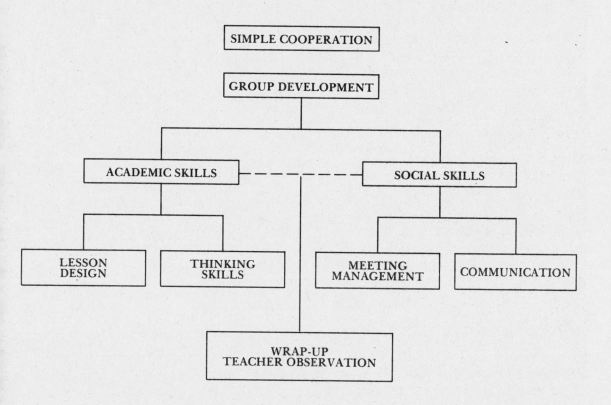

As students progress in group skills, they participate in STU-DENT SETTING STANDARDS and are introduced to practices which teach COMPLETING THE TASK. Because Simple Cooperation classes develop such high degrees of trust and support, the trauma of ending the class is eased with BREAKING UP ACTIVITIES. We will explain all of these and other group development techniques in detail.

CONFLICT

Conflict in the classroom is usually seen as negative and frightening — it means TROUBLE — and some teachers immediately envision loss of authority, and classroom control and chaos. If we're honest about conflict we have to admit that it occurs in most classrooms. The Simple Cooperation classroom is no exception. Conflict can erupt at any time in the group process. But with the Simple Cooperation model, conflict becomes a source of growth. Conflict, in fact, is a natural part of group growth and without it there can be little or no change.

Conflict is a source of growth

DO NOT ASSUME THAT CONFLICT IS NEGATIVE!

Later, in the section on Group Development, we will show how to turn conflict from a negative to a positive; how to use it to teach students essential problem solving and brainstorming skills. You will learn specific strategies for confronting conflict in a variety of situations and activites that will engage your students in resolving problems instead of engaging in conflict.

Turn conflict from a negative to a positive

GROUPS AND GROUP ROLES

Within the larger group of the class, the Simple Cooperation model uses smaller cooperative groups for each lesson. Each lesson has both an academic and a social objective; very simple ones at first, progressing only as each level is mastered. Within this small group framework, the students learn group roles. These help the group stay on task, give feedback, measure achievement and prepare the group product, while teaching each member the skills demanded by the group roles:

Each lesson has both an academic and a social objective

* selective and attentive listening;
* giving and receiving praise;
* clarifying information; and
* other group roles

Each student may be given an individual grade or reward for the lesson, and/or the group as a whole may be graded and rewarded for successfully working together.

It is not necessary to change your whole teaching approach at once to begin realizing the benefits of Simple Cooperation. In fact, we recommend choosing just one academic area at first. If you're an elementary teacher, choose a subject area that traditionally lends itself to group activities; such as science, social studies or history. Secondary teachers might choose to begin Simple Cooperation in one class period only.

Not necessary to change your whole teaching approach

As with any new process, academic and preparation time might appear to be lost in the beginning as you and your students are learning Simple Cooperation techniques. It will take longer at first to prepare lessons, and certainly more class time to complete a given assignment. There may be times in the first few weeks when you wonder why you got into this! After a while the frustration will lessen. Designing a Simple Cooperation lesson will become second nature. And you will be rewarded by seeing your students exhibiting a high degree of on-task behavior and group skills.

In the beginning it will take longer to prepare lessons

As the process of Simple Cooperation is embedded, learning will accelerate markedly. As workshop leaders, even we have sometimes been surprised at the speed of this phenomenon. There seem to be several reasons for it. First, a multi-modality approach to instruction is built into each Simple Cooperation lesson. Students are talking and listening to each other as well as reading and writing the lesson material. In most cases it's no longer necessary to design lessons to meet individual student modality strengths. Second, the time that students are actively involved in learning is extremely high and each student has a vested interest in completing the task that goes beyond him/herself — each also has a commitment to the group. And third, Simple Cooperation brings an element into the learning process that we call teaching thinking skills.

Learning will accelerate

Multi-modality approach

Each student has a commitment to the group

TEACHING THINKING SKILLS

Teaching thinking skills

This element of the Simple Cooperation method involves teaching thought processes, or paths of thinking. Sometimes our low and middle range learners can't accomplish a task because they've never thought of a way to do it. Sometimes our high range and gifted students accomplish a task but have no notion of how they did it. Teaching thinking skills helps fill in the gaps by giving the students an inner dialogue, an interior script of the necessary thinking process to which they can refer the next time they have a similar task to accomplish.

Inner dialogue

In understanding this concept it might help to think of this inner dialogue as analogous to a computer program. The computer (and student) has the capacity to do a given task. But until it is programmed — is given a way of sorting and putting the information together — both capacity and information available for input are useless. Until the student has learned a way of sorting and putting information together he/she can't complete the task.

Sometimes teaching thinking skills is nothing more than explaining something that seems to be "obvious" but which a student has somehow not learned or been taught. Sometimes this process is considerably more subtle and requires demonstration of relationships and transference of previously learned information. For example, a sixth grade student we once taught was reading on a second grade level. She was a bright, likeable youngster who obviously had the capacity to be a good reader. She had the information she needed for reading. Year after year she'd been taught the phonetic sounds of letters, and tested 100% on sounding them out.

Transference of previously learned information

She had been able to learn some words by sight; a skill that had helped maintain her sanity up to this point. Her reading problem remained a mystery until we began talking to her about how she went about the task of decoding words phonetically — and discovered that she simply didn't. The concept of blending phonetic sounds into whole words had never been explained, thus it never entered her internal dialogue.

She easily grasped the concept of blending. Now, with a process to use, she improved her reading skills by several grade levels in just a few months.

Teaching thinking skills, in the Simple Cooperation model, helps students like this who lack an inner dialogue or verbal road map to reach a solution. It also helps students who DO use an inner process but find it difficult to explain what that process is, and therefore can't extend it consciously to other tasks.

Gifted students often have this problem. They just "know" the answer but have no idea how they got it. This works alright for them in school, but it becomes a handicap later, in university and work situations. In life after high school they will need to be able to transfer and use their thinking skills for creativity and problem solving.

Gifted students

The Simple Cooperation model helps high, low and middle range students when they work together in cooperative groups. Using Simple Cooperation, sharing of skills becomes a group strength that benefits all students. It provides a consistent, ongoing forum for sharing thinking skills processes. And the task of teaching these thinking skills is no longer solely yours as teacher — it's shared by the class as a whole.

Helps high, middle and low range achievers

TEACHERS AND SIMPLE COOPERATION

At the core of the Simple Cooperation model is that you, the teacher, become a FACILITATOR of learning as opposed to being an "expert" who stands in front of the class DISSEMINATING facts and information. As a facilitator you become a guide, provide direction, help draw out the strengths of each student to accomplish the group objectives. Being a teacher/facilitator gives you the time to do what most of us like best about teaching —getting involved with the students.

Teacher, the facilitator of learning

While the concept of teacher-as-facilitator is fundamental to the Simple Cooperation model, it does not take the place of direct teaching. The difference is more in how you perceive your role as a teacher, than in eliminating direct teaching. New information must always be taught. There are always times when the "teacher as expert" role is necessary. Relying exclusively on this role as a teacher, however, robs your students of the chance to think for

Does not take the place of direct teaching

themselves — to discover information on their own, make connections, share knowledge, formulate questions. By combining the traditional and facilitation roles, you will vastly increase your effectiveness as a teacher, and your students' abilities as learners.

Students think for themselves

LAYING THE FOUNDATION

The following chapters talk about aspects of communication and group development which are usually ignored in the context of classrooms, and how these relate to the Simple Cooperation model. Then we will share with you various ways we have developed (and gathered from workshop participants) for putting this knowledge to work in teaching actual lessons. Finally, we offer sample lesson plans and activities for each of the major components of implementing Simple Cooperation.

Some of the concepts here may be familiar to you — others may be new. If you find yourself somewhat at sea at first, be patient; it will come together in time, and be more than worth your efforts.

SUMMARY OF KEY POINTS

• Simple Cooperation results in students focusing on the assigned task.

• Simple Cooperation integrates social and academic skills.

• The development of social skills is critical for present and future success.

• Simple Cooperation establishes a safe, secure and supportive environment.

• The group development process involves several stages: Setting Standards, Getting Acquainted, Students Setting Standards, Completing The Task, Breaking-up.

• Simple Cooperation provides a natural setting for teaching thinking skills.

CHAPTER 2
COMMUNICATION

OVERVIEW

This chapter discusses the four major areas of communication and points out that the two most used in everyday life, listening and speaking, are the least taught in public schools.

Effective speaking and listening techniques, and nonverbal messages, are explained in depth. A suggested teaching sequence is provided within the text.

The student's success in the classroom, at play, in interpersonal relationships, and later in the working world all depend on his/her ability to communicate well. Your effectiveness as a teacher is also dependent upon your skill as a communicator.

There are four basic communication skills: reading, writing, listening and speaking. Schools normally teach these skills in reverse order of their importance in the student's life. The most taught are reading and writing, the least taught are listening and speaking; more time spent speaking than reading, and more time reading than writing. With Simple Cooperation we bring these all-important skills of listening and speaking into their proper place in the curriculum. We also include study and practice of nonverbal communication — another element of communication which is largely ignored in the classroom, yet vastly important in life. The Simple Cooperation model teaches these communication skills through specific activities, but it will be obvious as you go along that attention to communication skills is a part of all classroom activity.

Four communication skills

Because communication skills have been so widely ignored as subjects of study, we'll first explore some of the concepts and elements of sending and receiving messages; what these skills are, how they work, what sometimes stops them from working. Once you have this background, we'll show how Simple Cooperation helps you teach communication through specific activities. Finally, in Section II, you will find sample activities to help you put what you've learned to work in your classroom.

Communication skills have been ignored

It may not be necessary to point out that you, as teacher and model of good communication skills, will be examining these skills in yourself in some depth. You will be looking hard, perhaps for the first time, at how well you send and receive messages yourself. A caution: for many people this is very threatening. We're not certain exactly why — perhaps in looking closely at our own communication techniques, we find that we're not as effective as we'd always thought. It can be upsetting to discover that our own communication skills can be dramatically improved. The teacher must be aware of this possibility in him/herself and in students, particularly at the secondary level when young egos are fragile.

Teacher, a model of good communication

You can help yourself and your students by concentrating on improving your communication skills rather than wasting energy in feeling bad about your "inadequacy." These skills can and will improve through use of the Simple Cooperation model.

Improving communication skills

WHAT IS COMMUNICATION?

Effective communication is defined as the transference of ideas, thoughts, attitudes and opinions from a sender (speaker) to a receiver (listener), with the receiver understanding the content of the message in the same manner that the sender intended. Thus, there are two principal parties in a communication transaction — the sender and the receiver (Figure 2). It's common to regard these as active and passive roles, respectively; but as we will see, both are active roles, and both can be improved through proper teaching.

Effective communication defined

A communication begins when one person sends a message to another. Messages are traditionally divided into two types — verbal and nonverbal, and for lack of better ones, we will use these terms here. However, it is important to understand that there is really no such thing as an exclusively verbal message. A spoken message always has behavior attached to it; such as tone of voice, inflection, tempo, volume, facial expression, body posture, breathing rhythm, etc. Even pupil size and perspiration can be part of a so-called "verbal" message — or they can stand alone and convey a message quite effectively all on their own.

Verbal and nonverbal messages

A person might confront you with a flushed face and compressed

Figure 2. Major components of Effective Communication.

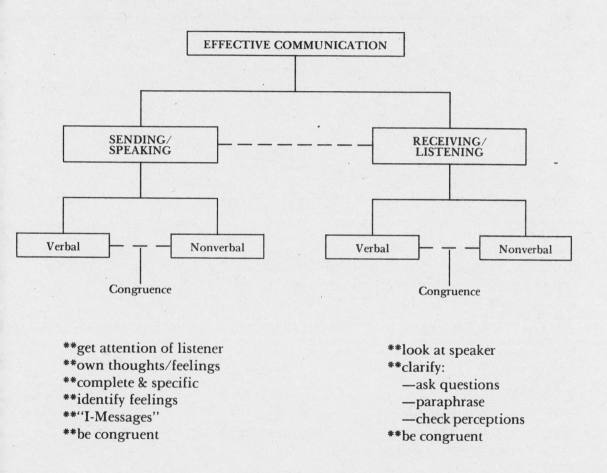

**get attention of listener
**own thoughts/feelings
**complete & specific
**identify feelings
**"I-Messages"
**be congruent

**look at speaker
**clarify:
 —ask questions
 —paraphrase
 —check perceptions
**be congruent

lips, breathing rapidly through the nose, eyebrows drawn together over glaring eyes and fists clenched at the sides — OR he/she might say, in a flat monotone voice with clipped words "You miserable so and so, you make me absolutely furious." Both are very effective communications.

For our purposes here, when we use the term "verbal" we will mean the spoken words of a message, and "nonverbal" to indicate all the other ways that messages can be transmitted. But bear in mind the relationship between the two — we'll be discussing it in more depth later on.

Verbal vs. nonverbal

SENDING MESSAGES — THE "SPEAKER"

The first step in sending a message is to get the receiver's attention. The simplest way to do this is to say the receiver's name. If the response doesn't clearly indicate that the receiver is ready to be attentive — if he/she simply grunts or nods without looking up — it might take some further phrase: "Do you have a minute?" Getting the listener's attention may seem almost too obvious to mention, yet many people launch into their main message without doing so. Before the listener understands she/he is being addressed, much of the message has already been said. Taking a moment to establish the listener's attention also gives him/her time to stop thinking about whatever else was going on and refocus on the message about to be received.

Getting the receivers attention

It is also important to establish eye contact with the receiver if at all possible. Not only does this signal the real attention of the receiver, it permits the nonverbal part of the message to be sent; the gestures, facial expressions, etc., that emphasize and illuminate the verbal part of the message. (More of this later.) A caution here, though: in some cultures it is considered disrespectful for a youngster to have direct eye contact with an adult. It is IMPERATIVE that the teacher BE AWARE OF AND SENSITIVE TO THE CULTURAL DIFFERENCES OF THE STUDENTS THEY TEACH!

Establishing eye contact

The next step in sending effective messages is to own your thoughts, ideas and feelings. We tend to talk about 'THEM' a lot — 'THEY say', it's up to 'THEM'. Have you ever wondered who 'they' and 'them' are? So often we seem to be afraid to say "I

Owning thoughts, ideas and feelings

think" or "My idea is..." or "I feel." Students need a great deal of practice and reinforcement to own their thoughts, etc.

THE "3-Cs" — BE CLEAR, CONCISE, COMPLETE

Effective sending/speaking requires learning how to state a message clearly, concisely and completely. First you must give the receiver the necessary background information to understand your message. Before launching into the main message, the sender should provide a context for the information to follow. Children often omit this step. Surely all of us have had to stop a student in the middle of an excited rush of details about some incident and get them to say what they're talking about so we can understand their message.

Be clear, concise, complete

Children are not alone in sometimes failing to give proper background for a message. For example...Have you ever had someone tell you a fairly lengthy story which included several references to a particular person — say, someone named Eric. Try as you might, you can't remember who Eric is. From the way the speaker is talking, she/he seems to be taking it for granted that you'll know this Eric person. You listen for clues, and you'll rack your brain but you just can't identify the man.

Giving background for a message

Finally you give up and ask — only to learn that Eric is some friend of the speaker's whom you've never met. Had the speaker identified him first as "a friend of mine" you would have been able to relax and concentrate on the story. As it was, your attention was distracted as you tried to supply background information for yourself that should have been given by the speaker.

Too much background or detail can confuse a message, too. Remember, effective sending requires learning to state your message clearly and CONCISELY. You must say enough to let the listener know what's being talked about — but not so much that the main point of the message gets lost in excess detail, and the listener gets tired of waiting for you to get to the point.

Too much background

Being clear and concise not only enhances the listener's level of understanding but retains her/his interest in what is being said. A rule of thumb is to use only as many words as are required to get the message across. Extra words do nothing but confuse the issue.

The speaker should stick to one topic at a time, without jumping from one subject to another. The listener won't know what information belongs to which topic if the speaker wanders from one point to another. As the message proceeds, the speaker can and should check with the listener from time to time to determine if the message is being understood. This is particularly true when relating long or complex issues, instructions, reports or similar messages. A simple question such as: "Am I making sense?" or "Are you understanding (or following) all of this?" is all that's really needed. If the listener indicates that he/she is having difficulty understanding, the speaker can elaborate on the message, or rephrase it. The speaker can also use visual aids such as graphs, charts or other types of visual cues to assist the listener in understanding unusually complex messages.

Stick to one topic at a time

Check with the listener

EXPRESSING FEELINGS

The speaker should try to use words that say precisely what is meant, not vague or catchall terms or phrases. This is particularly true when expressing feelings. We have a tendency in our society to discount and/or deny our feelings. We tend to avoid calling them by name...saying clearly "I'm happy," or angry, or sad. Instead we use similes such as "I'm on cloud nine" or "I'm really down in the dumps today" or "I wanted to punch that guy out." It takes a great deal of practice and reinforcement to identify our feelings by name and to claim them as our own.

Naming feelings

CONFLICT OR POTENTIAL CONFLICT SITUATIONS

Many people have a tendency to simply blurt out their feelings. When we are angry, we may do so in an aggressive manner (intentionally or not). We also have a tendency to become defensive when we think we are being criticized or attacked. The result is usually a heated argument and bad feelings.

We can avoid unwanted and unnecessary argument and conflicts by stating our feelings in ways that will be least offensive to the listener.

We can avoid unwanted and unnecessary arguments

"I-messages," as developed and taught by Dr. Thomas Gordon of the Effectiveness Training Institute, are comprised of three specific and distinct parts: the feeling, the other's action or behavior

"I-messages"

which preceded the feeling; and the consequence of tangible effect. Example: A group member has failed to complete his/her part of an assignment. Typical reactions from other students may include name-calling or some other form of verbal aggression. An alternative communication strategy is an "I-message" which could be phrased like this: "I'm really angry that you did not complete your part of the assignment because our group paper is now incomplete and we will receive a lower grade."

The "I-message" tells the listener exactly how a person feels, why he/she feels that way, and what effect the listener's behavior has on the speaker. This type of statement is clear and focuses on behavior rather than an evaluation of the person's character; thus, it is less likely to result in a verbal fight.

(Note: "I-messages" may also be used in a positive manner — "I'm really proud that we've all completed our parts so well because we will surely receive a high grade for our paper.")

RECEIVING A MESSAGE — THE "LISTENER"

A good listener does more than passively receive the message being transmitted by the speaker. Remember that the definition of an effective communication is that the message be understood in the same way that the sender intended. The listener has a responsibility to help achieve this goal. Learning to be an active, skilled listener is as important as learning to be a good speaker. All of us listen more than we speak, read or write; yet listening techniques are rarely, if ever, taught the student in a systematic way that emphasizes the importance of these skills.

Good listener

Least taught

Simple Cooperation brings listening skills into their proper position of importance to the student. Learning them takes a great deal of practice, with regular, structured feedback from the teacher and other students. This is provided both through specific listening-skill activities and as an element in all other Simple Cooperation techniques.

The first task of the listener is to pay attention — to focus on the speaker and make a genuine effort to hear and understand the message. Listening, too often, takes the form of a game called "Hurry up and finish talking, it's my turn now." In this game

Task of listener

very little listening really occurs. The listener is not receiving the message at all, but simply marking time until the speaker is finished.

As the message proceeds, the listener must try to judge whether or not she/he really understands what's being said. If not, the listener has basically two choices: to guess or to clarify. Sometimes guesses are accurate; more often they aren't. Clarifying, which is a form of feedback, makes a lot more sense than guessing. The Simple Cooperation model teaches listener feedback in a variety of ways.

One method of clarifying is to simply ask questions. In the example given earlier, where the listener couldn't identify the person being talked about in the long anecdote, a simple question early on in the story would have clarified everything. "I'm sorry, I can't figure out which Eric you mean — is it someone I know?"

Clarifying

Students often don't ask questions because they're afraid to appear "dumb." It's up to the teacher to establish a safe environment for questioning, and encourage students to ask for clarification. This means that the teacher must be careful not to demonstrate any behavior, verbal or nonverbal, that can be interpreted as non-accepting of questions. Statements such as "Finish your workbook, of course! What did you think?" and signals of impatience such as raised eyebrows, rolling eyes, smirks, looks of irritation or exasperated signs all give the student the clear message that a "dumb" question has been asked.

Ask questions

Students model teacher behavior. If the teacher demonstrates non-accepting behavior when questions are asked, two things will happen: students will feel free to ridicule the questioner...and students will stop asking questions.

Another clarifying technique is paraphrasing. In paraphrasing, the listener states in her/his own words the way in which she/he has INTERPRETED OR UNDERSTOOD the message. Note that paraphrasing is NOT simply restating the message in different words — this wouldn't guarantee clarity. For example, consider the following exchange:

Paraphrasing

Teacher 1: "David shouldn't be in this classroom."

Teacher 2:   "You're right, he really shouldn't be in this room."

Are we certain they both have the same idea about David? Perhaps they think they are talking about the same thing but it's more likely they aren't which they would have discovered if Teacher 2 had paraphrased instead of restated:

Teacher 1:   "David shouldn't be in this classroom."

Teacher 2:   "You mean that he's such a troublemaker he disrupts the whole class?"

Teacher 1:   "Oh, no, it's that David is so far advanced that I'm having trouble challenging his mind."

Teacher 2:   "Oh, I see what you mean."

In the second dialogue, using paraphrasing to clarify the message, a clear communication has occurred. To better understand the difference between restating and paraphrasing, it might help to remember that restating is a tool for the SENDER of a message — to ensure that the message is sent clearly by saying it in different words. Paraphrasing is a tool used by the RECEIVER of a message, to check that his/her understanding of the message is what the sender intended.

Restating vs. paraphrasing

A third clarifying technique is to 'check out' your perceptions. This is important when the listener is unsure of the feelings of the speaker or thinks she/he is getting a double message. Since this concerns primarily nonverbal communication, it is discussed at length in the next few pages.

Checking perceptions

The consequences for failing to clarify an unclear message can be severe: "You must finish your book by Tuesday," may seem clear enough to the teacher, who means the workbook in the Science Class. To the student who guesses wrongly that the book meant is the textbook, failure to clarify the message can be disastrous come next Tuesday.

NONVERBAL COMMUNICATION

We've referred to nonverbal messages already, and defined them as all parts of a message except the spoken words. Depending on which researcher you read, somewhere between 70% and 85% of our communication is nonverbal. Yet schools seldom teach stu-

Nonverbal messages

dents what nonverbal communication is or how it relates to the spoken word.

Earlier we listed some kinds of nonverbal communication: tone of voice, inflection, tempo, volume, facial expression, body posture, breathing rhythm, flushed face, pupil size and perspiration rate. To this list may be added gesture, eye movement, non-word vocalization...any and all behavior during a communication other than the spoken words.

Note that much of what we refer to as nonverbal involves the spoken message: the way in which words are delivered. Tempo, volume, inflection, etc. are nonverbal components of the verbal message. (Also note that nonverbal communication is NOT synonymous with "body language", although language is certainly one aspect of nonverbal communication.)

It is virtually impossible to communicate without giving nonverbal messages. Even an attempt to do so contains a nonverbal message! A speaker with a quiet face, still body, even respiration and even, monotonal delivery of words is giving a definite nonverbal message by the very act of trying not to. The speaker may be trying to project utter sincerity, or to direct attention to the verbal message, or refusing to share his/her emotional state for some reason...the possibilities are many.

Often we're not even aware of the messages we're giving nonverbally, and far too often these nonverbal messages are misinterpreted. But you may ask how can this be? Someone who's blushing is obviously embarrassed, right? It's easy to see that someone who closes her/his eyes during a conversation is simply not interested in what's being said, isn't it?

Often not aware of the messages we're giving

Really? Consider: Blushing does sometimes mean embarrassment. But some people blush when they're irritated, excited, hurt, or just overly warm. The person who closes his/her eyes during a conversation may be inattentive, tired, or simply concentrating on what's being said. A person whose eyes shift around when she/he speaks and who can't look you straight in the eye MAY be lying — but may just be embarrassed or very timid or unsure. A person who does the opposite may be telling the truth — or may just have learned to control her/his nonverbal behavior to

Interpreting messages

APPEAR honest.

WATCHING YOURSELF

If nonverbal signals can be so badly misinterpreted or used to manipulate, is there any way to avoid misunderstanding? Yes. Perhaps not perfectly, but there are several ways to greatly improve clarity and understanding, for both listener/receiver and speaker/sender.

Begin with yourself. Without trying to change it at first, begin paying attention to your own nonverbal behavior. What signals do you give when you're anxious? When you're happy, sad, depressed, annoyed with a friend, or feeling insecure? Do you cover embarrassment with a steady string of words, and avert your eyes and blush? When do you speak loudly or softly, faster or slower? Do you sometimes isolate yourself from a group with subtle body movement?

Begin with yourself
Nonverbal signals

As a receiver, how do you find yourself signaling your interest, or lack of it? Do you look intently at the speaker and use nonverbal sounds and nods to indicate your attention and understanding? When you doodle as you listen, does that mean you're bored or that you listen better when your hands are busy?

After you've observed your own nonverbal behavior for a while and answered some of these questions, ask a friend to tell you how you react in these situations. You may have to reassure your friend that you really do want honest feedback — that you promise not to be insulted or offended by their response. (And then, notice how you go about doing that. What's your facial expression, tone, body posture, as you emphasize your sincerity?)

Ask a friend

You may be surprised at what you learn. All of us use nonverbal behaviors we're not aware of. You may learn that some of yours are causing you to be misunderstood, but that others are felt to be effective and attractive. "I can always tell when you're nervous because you nod your head a lot and talk loud." Or: "One of the things I like about you is that you really pay attention when I talk. You smile when you understand a point, and I can tell you're puzzled when you frown and cock your head."

Once we've checked our own nonverbal behavior by self-observation and with a trusted friend, we can begin to change those things that have become bad habits, and are keeping us from being good communicators. We can also begin to see more clearly how the nonverbal behavior of others can be interpreted in many different ways.

CHECK IT OUT

Watch your students and think about what they're telling you with their nonverbal language. What is the "obnoxious" child really feeling? Or the student who goes off by himself at recess? How about that child who swaggers and brags, or the one who rarely speaks up in class or in groups? Is the baggart really so sure of her/himself, or does the nonverbal behavior mask an inner insecurity? Is the quiet child really timid, or is she/he simply absorbed in what's being said?

Adults too seldom check their perceptions about a child to determine what the child is really feeling. We don't know if it's because adults think they KNOW what the child is feeling better than the child does, or if adults consider it beneath them to check with the youngster. We DO know that very few teachers take the time to discern the student's real feelings.

Checking perceptions

You can help your students, even very young ones, learn about nonverbal language. One way to do this is to check out your perceptions with them. "It sounds like you're really hurt. Is that true?" "I get the impression that you're confused. Are you?" "Your face is flushed. Does that mean you're embarrassed or angry?" "You're frowning and shaking your head. Is there something bothering you?" "It looks like you're not happy. Is that true?"

Helping students learn

When checking out your perceptions, avoid jumping to conclusions or interpreting the child's behavior according to your own assumptions about the reason for it. Don't forget that nonverbal behavior can easily be misinterpreted. If you are fairly certain about the child's feelings, you can offer a guess. But be sure that you leave room for the child to correct your guess if it's wrong.

Primary-age children often don't know the words that accurately describe their feelings. We spoke earlier of the importance of

Primary-age children

calling feelings by their right names. When checking your perceptions, as above, be sure to offer words appropriate to grade level if the child doesn't seem to know them.

This technique of checking your perceptions of nonverbal behavior accomplishes a great deal. By doing so you've avoided making assumptions about the child that may be wrong, you've brought nonverbal behavior to the child's attention in a non-threatening way, you've helped the child clarify and name the feeling, and you've modeled the process for them.

The complete communication process, including checking perceptions, is reflected in Figure 3.

CONGRUENCE AND INCONGRUENCE

Now we come to another kind of relationship between verbal and nonverbal languages: that of congruence or incongruence. Congruence means that the two kinds of messages appear to be the same; both words and actions seem to be expressing the same thing. Incongruence is the opposite: the speaker's words may say one thing, while nonverbal clues indicate quite another.

When verbal and nonverbal messages are incongruent the listener is forced to make a choice. Which message shall I, the listener, believe; or should I not believe either one? Most often it is the nonverbal message that is believed.

Verbal and nonverbal congruence

For example...Your new site administrator has assured the faculty that she/he is there to help and support you; that if you have a problem you can't seem to resolve you have only to make an appointment and he/she will be happy to explore alternative solutions with you. Later, you do have a problem with a student and you seek the guidance of your principal. He/she welcomes you into the office and five minutes later, as you're relating the specifics surrounding the problem, she/he begins shuffling papers on the desk and glancing at the clock. You ask if he/she is too busy now and should you make another appointment. The principal curtly assures you that she/he is not too busy and really wants to help you.

Are you going to believe the words or the nonverbal cues?

Which will you believe?

Figure 3. COMMUNICATION PROCESS

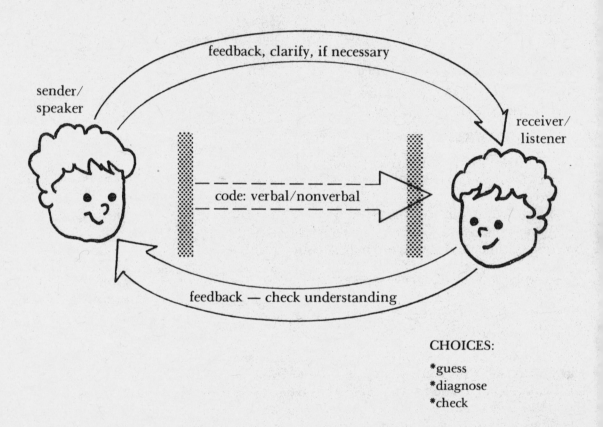

NOTE: The shaded areas reflect perceptual zones...each message, verbal or nonverbal, must travel through each individual's perceptual zone which is comprised of attitudes, opinions, knowledge, thoughts, values, feelings, and previous experiences. These and many other variables result in each person's perception and interpretation of what any given behavior or verbal message means. It is easy to see how a message may be misinterpreted. The listener must, in fact, decode what the speaker intends to say; checking the accuracy of your interpretation becomes critical in many situations. It is equally important for the speaker to verify the listener's perceptions/interpretation or to clarify by restating the message if the receiver is not "getting it".

We give such incongruent messages for many reasons. Lack of awareness about our own feelings is one, and fear of expressing them honestly is another. Fear of embarrassment or pain is a powerful motive for trying to conceal feelings. Many of us are afraid that expressing our real feelings will make us vulnerable. We suspect that people may not like us as we really are and we'll end up with no friends. Or we're afraid of being ridiculed or seeming stupid. So we say one thing with our words and another with our nonverbal signals, hoping to avoid the things we fear will happen if we're honest.

We also try to hide feelings that we know are "wrong." We might know that we're "supposed" to be patient and calm in a situation but what we really feel is frustration and intense irritation. The response we give to the second or third student who interrupts our concentration on paperwork might be genuinely patient and calm. The response to the tenth student might be given in the same words, but our narrowed lips and exasperated sign give quite another message. You may be sure that the child will believe the latter message, not your words.

Trying to hide feelings

Since a major source of incongruent verbal and nonverbal communication is fear, it is imperative for the teacher to create and foster a safe and secure environment for students. In a Simple Cooperation classroom, standards of behavior are established very early, and we will be presenting specific guidelines for this later. These standards must include as fundamental that each and every individual in the class be accepted and respected as she/he is. No one should ever be allowed to ridicule or demean another. You, the teacher, must model this behavior and help enforce these rules. Students must not be permitted to laugh at other students or call them names. Should this happen, you must take the offender aside and firmly state that this is not allowed in this classroom. If this problem is pervasive with the group it would be appropriate to add: "Treat class members with respect" to the group standards, and to teach this skill to the group.

Fear

POWERFUL LISTENING

Earlier we said that listening is an active role in a communication, not a passive one. Nonverbal language may be the listener's

Listening, an active role

single most powerful tool for achieving good communication. A "good listener" is highly prized, and what makes a good listener is often the way in which he/she signals interest and attention by the use of nonverbal language. Eye contact, nodding, vocalization, and other signals assure the speaker that she/he is being understood and that the listener values what he/she is saying. A frown or cocked head lets the speaker know that something isn't being understood, and is an implied request for clarification.

When working with younger children, getting to the same eye level as the child is a good nonverbal assurance of attention. It's often an excellent technique to crouch, sit in chairs side by side, or even set the child on a desk or table so that the two of you talk at the same eye level.

Nonverbal assurance of attention

You can help encourage good nonverbal listening habits by remarking on them and praising them, in addition to modeling them. "Suzanne, I like it when you nod and smile like that. It lets me know that I really got through to you."

TEACHING EFFECTIVE COMMUNICATION

Since communication skills have not been widely taught, particularly listening and nonverbal communication, even older students may need instruction on a very basic, simple level. Teaching communication skills can begin with very young children, and continue with increasing depth and subtlety throughout secondary school.

Where to begin instruction

Whatever the skill-level or age of your students, it is important that only one aspect of a skill be taught at a time, and thoroughly mastered before moving on to another. You'll find a suggested continuum of communication skills at the end of this chapter (Figure 4) — but note that it should be used as a guideline only. Your own perceptions of the group's skill level and needs will be the best guide to the order in which to introduce new skills.

As we stressed earlier, it is critical that the classroom be a safe, secure, accepting environment where students are encouraged to ask questions and to reveal their feelings without fear of ridicule or embarrassment. We've also given several techniques for giving and receiving feedback about communication skills. Feedback is

Feedback

the most important tool in teaching communication skills, but it can be dangerous unless you are careful and firm about its use. You must constantly demonstrate and reinforce the rule that feedback is meant to HELP the receiver, not to criticize or belittle her/him. The person giving feedback should never be allowed to use it as a means of making him/herself feel more important or a better person. You'll find many activities and techniques in Section II that will help establish and reinforce the proper environment and attitudes for teaching communciation skills.

SUMMARY OF KEY POINTS

• Communication skills are usually ignored as specific subjects of study in the public schools.

• Verbal messages always include nonverbal messages.

• Techniques for sending effective messages include: getting the attention of the intended receiver; being clear, concise and complete; identifying feelings by name; using "I-messages" in conflict situations; using visual aids to clarify complex messages; and demonstrating congruence between the verbal and nonverbal messages.

• Effective listening techniques include: attending to the speaker; clarifying by asking questions, paraphrasing, checking your perceptions of the sender's nonverbal messages.

• More than 70% of all communication is nonverbal, thus it is critical to be aware of one's own nonverbal messages and to check your perception of others' nonverbal cues.

• A communication skills continuum was provided as a guide for sequencing instruction of effective communication techniques.

Figure 4. COMMUNICATION CONTINUUM

SENDING:

1. GET LISTENER'S ATTENTION
2. OWN THOUGHTS, IDEAS, FEELINGS
3. '3 Cs' — BE CLEAR, CONCISE, COMPLETE
4. IDENTIFY FEELINGS BY NAME
5. NONVERBAL AWARENESS
6. CONGRUENCE: VERBAL/NONVERBAL
7. "I-MESSAGES"

LISTENING:

1. LOOK AT SPEAKER
2. CLARIFY BY ASKING QUESTIONS
3. CLARIFY BY PARAPHRASING
4. PERCEPTION CHECKING
5. NONVERBAL AWARENESS
6. CONGRUENCE

CHAPTER 3
YOU, YOUR CLASS AND GROUP DEVELOPMENT

OVERVIEW

This chapter discusses, in sequence, the various stages necessary for the development of a cohesive, productive group.

Conflict, an inherent aspect of the group development process, may erupt at any time. A problem solving model is described and recommended as a way of dealing with conflict-type situations.

When people come together; be it as a faculty, a scout troup or a class, a group is formed. Some groups come together as a cohesive unit and some do not. Some groups remain just a collection of individuals in the same space, never seeming to agree on anything, never establishing supportive relationships, and often failing to accomplish their purpose as a group. The students gathered in your classroom form a group. Let's look at some of the basic elements and stages of group development in terms of the classroom group. (Figure 5 graphically presents an overview of the stages of the group development process.)

What is a group?

SETTING STANDARDS

All groups set their own standards of behavior. Lacking a set of rules from an organization or leader, the group will develop its own, usually through trial and error. Members will "try on" different behaviors to see what works and what doesn't work with this particular group of people. Behaviors are then modified according to the response of other members.

Groups set standards

The pattern of trying out and modifying behaviors is repeated many times until the class has developed a mutural definition of acceptable behavior.

Student-student standards will be established and, since the teacher is also a member of the group, student-teacher standards. The teacher is, sometimes unwittingly a full participant in the process by virtue of his/her acceptance or rejection of tried-out behaviors.

Figure 5

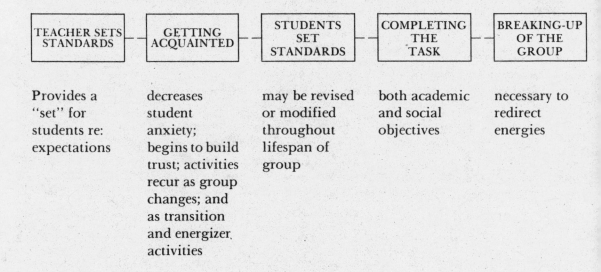

STAGES of CLASSROOM GROUP DEVELOPMENT				
TEACHER SETS STANDARDS	GETTING ACQUAINTED	STUDENTS SET STANDARDS	COMPLETING THE TASK	BREAKING-UP OF THE GROUP
Provides a "set" for students re: expectations	decreases student anxiety; begins to build trust; activities recur as group changes; and as transition and energizer activities	may be revised or modified throughout lifespan of group	both academic and social objectives	necessary to redirect energies

← — — — — ← — — — — POSSIBLE CONFLICT — — — — → — — — — →

(NOTE: The sequential stages of the group development process occur and recur throughout the group's lifetime. Group members continually become acquainted, each time at a different awareness level. Also, whenever a member leaves the group or a new member joins, the group, in effect, changes. This change requires additional "getting acquainted" processes. Standards will be revised as the group becomes more cohesive and as the group changes its composition.)

This laissez-faire method of setting standards does not produce the most coherent, productive classroom group. The first task in teaching effective group development, therefore, is to set standards as a conscious, directed process. The teacher, as the classroom leader, takes the initiative.

Laissez-faire method

In the Simple Cooperation model the teacher first establishes a baseline of behaviors: SETTING STANDARDS. These come from community norms and values, school rules, and the teacher's personal preferences and limitations — what she/he can "live with." Since it is important that standards be clearly articulated and consciously adopted, they should be written on a chart and presented as a "given" to the students. Each standard becomes a social skill objective in and of itself. While presented as a whole on the first day of class and covered in overview fashion, each should then be taught as a separate lesson.

Teacher setting standards

SUGGESTED STANDARDS INCLUDE:

Suggested standards

1. BE ON TIME
   This means that each student is responsible for being in his/her seat or work area as the schedule indicates. For lower elementary students, a chart of expected times may be posted on which are pictures of clocks; with upper grade students, a chart of times should be posted.

2. BE RESPONSIBLE FOR YOUR OWN LEARNING
   If a student has a question about an assignment she/he has the responsibility to ask that question first of another group member or members. If no one in the group knows the answer, he/she should then ask the teacher. A question should never go unanswered. A class member should never say, "I didn't know what to do."

Questions

3. BE RESPONSIBLE FOR YOUR OWN MATERIALS AND ASSIGNMENTS
   Each student has a responsibility to him/herself and the class as a whole, as well as his/her group members to carry his/her own share. She/he doesn't wait for someone else to remember for him/her. A clear procedure should be posted for students regarding access to materials and books to assist students in

actualizing this responsibility.

4. ONLY ONE PERSON CAN SPEAK AT A TIME

    This is the beginning step in teaching communication and meeting management skills. It cannot be assumed that this basic socialization skill has already been internalized regardless of grade level. The message that is given when this skill is emphasized is that in this classroom we will respect each individual's contribution to the group product.

    Beginning step in teaching communication

5. KEEP YOUR WORK AND DESK AREA CLEAN

    Each person is responsible for both her/his own personal space and the areas that everyone uses. It must be demonstrated what "clean" means in your classroom because a clean work space to one person may seem messy to another.

GETTING ACQUAINTED

When students enter a new classroom for the first time in a small school they may already know all or most of the students. In larger schools they may only recognize a face or two. That first day in a new class may be a frightening experience. Helping the students get acquainted with you and with each other sets the stage for everything to come in the class and for this newly formed group.

Frightening experience

Often, of course, in a class in which behavioral standards are set informally, by trial and error, that process itself is a big part of student getting acquainted activities. There is competition for control, measuring of each others' skills or clothes or level of anxiety, resulting in a set of attitudes and interaction patterns which are difficult or impossible to alter later. When you set standards consciously and provide getting acquainted activities, this poor beginning is avoided.

The students will begin to know you as a teacher as you present the standards, and as you describe the basic "housekeeping" procedures of the class. This must be done clearly, and the students should be encouraged to ask questions if they don't understand or if you've left something out. Students who are familiar with the basics of school and classroom life are less anxious, and function more smoothly as a group.

Students begin to know the teacher

The Getting Acquainted Activities and variations of those activities in the form of transition and energizing activities, presented in Section II, are then used to ease the students' initial reserve and shyness and to begin accustoming them to working in a group at a single activity.

Getting acquainted activities

STUDENTS SETTING STANDARDS

With a very young group, the baseline standards set by the teacher will be all that's necessary for a while. As the class matures as a group, and with older students, the students should actively participate in setting group standards. Within the first several weeks of class, after the original set of standards have been taught and mastered by the students, it's appropriate to review the standards with them. You might ask them whether they feel that additional standards are needed, or to suggest changes as required.

As the group matures

Discussion of standards should be done within the context of the class's central purpose. All groups come together for a purpose. This may range from having a good time to running the United Nations. The purpose of the classroom group is to maximize the potential of each student to learn the social and academic skills that will lead to a happy, productive life. Discussion should be based on whether or not the standard will help or hinder this goal.

Central purpose

This may be done any time during the school year. We suggest that the first formal class input session about standards be done after the class has become acquainted with each other and with you. Later on in smaller Simple Cooperation groups, students will become quite adept at setting "mini-group" standards, based on the goal of the particular small group.

COMPLETING THE TASK

Completing the task, whether it be academic or otherwise, is the next progressive stop in the sequence. Productivity will be greatly enhanced when you take the time to first lead your students through the standard setting and getting acquainted stages of the group development process. A suggested lesson plan format, sample lessons, and activities are found in Section II to assist you in developing Simple Cooperation lessons.

BREAKING UP

There comes a time for each group to break up. This can be a difficult time for students in a Simple Cooperation class, and make them feel sad when it comes time for the group to disband. Conflict frequently erupts as the school year draws to an end. Ironically, the very success of the Simple Cooperation classroom in building a close, effective, supportive group contributes to the possibility of conflict. Remember, these students entered the classroom on the first day of school not knowing exactly what to expect or exactly how they would be accepted. Since then they've been members of a cohesive group built on mutual trust, respect and caring. Now they must leave the safety and good feeling of the group.

Difficult time for students

The teacher can and should help them through their feelings of loss and anxiety with carefully planned group breaking up activities. Examples of these are given in Section II. Many of the Transition Activities, which are also found in Section II, are good for this period, as well. When there is conflict, it is important to deal with it as a problem to be solved using the methods the students have learned. More about conflict and problem solving later in this section.

Carefully planned activities

GROUP GROWTH AND MATURITY

Groups, like people, progress through phases of development. Within each stage a certain level of maturity must be reached and consolidated before the group can go on to the next. While perfection isn't required and indeed, students may be working on several stages at one time, moving too fast through the stages may be counterproductive. If the group tries to jump to a new phase before it has mastered the earlier phases it may have trouble. One sign of an immature group is lack of productivity in accomplishing its task. We're all familiar with the committee that never seems to be able to reach a decision or produce any action. It just meets and meets and meets, endlessly circling the same questions and meeting the same blocks.

Perfection isn't required

Sign of an immature group

If the committee had paid attention to the need to get acquainted, to set standards for itself, to define its goals, it might have been more successful. When a classroom group isn't producing according to its goals, look to see if earlier stages have been skipped or imperfectly mastered. If necessary, go back and repeat earlier activities to eliminate the weak spots in the group's functioning.

The natural order of group development in the classroom will usually emerge if the fundamentals are securely mastered.

CONFLICT

Let us begin by repeating what we said earlier: DO NOT ASSUME THAT CONFLICT IS NEGATIVE. Conflict can certainly be unpleasant and uncomfortable while it lasts, but conflict brings change — and there is no growth or learning without change.

Conflict brings change

As teacher, we must involve ourselves in conflict resolution whether we like it or not. Very often we're placed in the position of making unilateral decisions in conflict situations — it's up to us to decide what to do and to enforce our decision. Do we call the parents? Suspend the students? Withhold a reward? Punish in some other way? Refer to the principal? Or simply talk with the students? How we approach a conflict situation and deal with it will determine whether the effect will be positive or negative.-..whether it will help pull the group together and make it grow, or create splits and tensions that will hold it back. Conflict brings emotion: anger, hurt, fear, embarrassment. Unresolved, it can continue, taking on new forms and resurfacing. But if we separate the feelings from the problem — the actual point(s) of disagreement — we can deal with the problem itself instead of just its symptoms.

Conflict positive or negative?

Conflict can resurface

Simple Cooperation offers ways of responding which translate conflict into problem solving, providing students with new skills to help them resolve conflict in present and future situations without sole dependence upon teacher intervention.

Problem solving

There are a number of situations which are referred to as conflict. Typically, these are times when two or more individuals strongly disagree and resort to verbal or even physical combat. Conflicts also erupt in competitive situations where there is only one prize for which more than one student is striving. A classic example is the class that is graded on a strict bell curve, with two percent of the class receiving A's, two percent F's and the rest falling somewhere in between.

Conflict is also situational — one person may see a heated exchange of words as a healthy argument while another person reacts to any disagreement with feelings of extreme discomfort. Environment also helps to define conflict situations: an interchange on the playground or in the hallway may seem perfectly appropriate, while the same interchange in the classroom would mean conflict.

Cultural and family emotional "styles" also confuse the issue of what is genuinely conflict and what is not. A perfectly normal "discussion" to some people may seem like a violent and threatening argument to others from different backgrounds or with different customs. *Cultural and family styles*

Whatever the circumstances, context or source of conflict, as teachers we are required to deal with it. The Simple Cooperation model provides a near-perfect vehicle for turning conflict into a positive force for learning and growth. Using the following problem solving and brainstorming techniques gives students practice and skill in working through conflict situations — a skill that is critical in their lives now and in the future. *Turning conflict into a positive force*

PROBLEM SOLVING

The problem solving techniques that follow are NOT used only or even primarily to resolve conflict. In fact, they might almost be better termed "Solution Finding" techniques, and they are as valuable in academic lessons as in social situations. The following model can be used when Cindy and Mike are quarreling about whose turn it is to be group Praiser — or they can be used by a social studies group to plan ways of completing a major history research project. *Problem solving*

The first step in the Simple Cooperation conflict model is to STATE THE PROBLEM: to write it down. This not only defines the situation that must be resolved, it helps to diffuse the emo- *Problem solving steps* tional content. Involve the group in defining the problem, whether the group is just two students with a disagreement, or the whole class with a challenge to meet.

For upper elementary students it's helpful to ask each student to write her/his own DEFINITION of the problem on a large piece of paper. Younger children could express their perceptions orally while the teacher writes them down. Identify the component parts of the issue, who and what is affected. Next, determine what conditions are preferred — what do you want to have in place of the current situation? Specify what must change.

Definition of the problem

Now help the students review and discuss the statements and decide which one or ones accurately express the REAL problem. You will need to help students clarify thoughts and facilitate the agreement process, particularly in the early stages of developing these skills. The next step in problem solving is to determine what the CONSTRAINTS to the solution are. How much time is available for resolving the problem? Who will make the final decision? Will that be you, the class as a whole, a sub-group in the class or...? What DECISION MAKING MODE will be used. (A discussion of these follows shortly.) It's helpful to list all the constraints on paper. Again, you need to take a very active role during this stage and, in fact, may need to make these decisions for the students at first. However — remember that the more you can involve those who will be affected by a decision in the decision making process, the more they will tend to support and agree with it. As much as possible, you should help the students learn the skills involved in decision making, so that they can perform these steps for themselves when that's appropriate.

The real problem

Constraints

Decision making mode

Once the problem has been STATED, the CONSTRAINTS defined, the DECISION MAKER identified and the DECISION MAKING MODE specified, the group can begin exploring solutions. This is done through "brainstorming."

BRAINSTORMING is a free-wheeling (but not chaotic) session in which students offer ideas — in this case the ideas are in search of a solution to a specific problem. Brainstorming is also an excellent way to generate ideas for other purposes. The rules for brainstorming are:

Brainstorming

Rules for brainstorming

— set and adhere to a specific amount of time for the brainstorming (3-5 minutes)

— write all ideas on a large piece of paper posted to the wall or on the chalkboard. EVERY idea is written down, no matter how "way out" it seems

— no evaluation of ideas is permitted during the idea-generating period — not even smiles, smirks, nods, "good," "ugh," etc.

After all ideas are listed, they are read aloud with any necessary clarification being given by the originator of the idea.

The second part of the brainstorming session involves evaluating the ideas. A very helpful tool in this evaluation is to graph them with the identified constraints. On another large sheet of paper, write the constraints across the top, at the head of a column for each one. Down the left side write each idea, one at a time, and invite the students to consider them in terms of each of the constraints. Make a check under each of the constraint items that the idea fits within. For example, if time is one of the constraints — a solution has to be accomplished, say, within two weeks —any idea which would take longer is not checked in the Time Constraint column. The idea(s) with the greatest number of checks then become the alternative solutions to be chosen among according to whichever decision making mode has been specified. These three steps are reflected in Figures 6.1, 6.2 and 6.3.

Evaluating ideas

Suggested activities for practicing brainstorming are included in Section II.

DECISION MAKING MODELS

It's important to teach students how to use various decision making models to give them flexibility in terms of processes at their command. We find the following four to be the most useful as they offer a range of approaches that ensures an appropriate model for most situations you are likely to encounter.

Decision making models

AUTOCRATIC: One person, unilaterally, makes the decision for all without taking input, ideas, suggestions, etc. This mode is based on the premise that one person knows what is best for the

Autocratic

group regardless of what group members think or feel. This is obviously the easiest model to use as decisions can be made very quickly. However, many people feel resentment at being controlled which is how they feel when they have no voice in the decision. People who do feel this way will simple ignore the decision or try to sabotage it.

DEMOCRATIC: Uses some form of voting, usually with a majority rule (it is critical to define what constitutes a "majority.") A potential draw-back with this model is that voting creates winners and losers. Very proud people often feel they've lost face if their favorite alternative was voted down. To save face they may just attempt to "prove" the decision was the wrong one and try to sabotage it.

Democratic

PARTICIPATORY: Everyone involved gives input to the ultimate decision maker, who considers the input when making the decision. It is important that genuine consideration of the input be given, so that this model isn't simply autocratic decision making wearing a false face.

Participatory

CONSENSUS: Everyone in the group participates on an equal level, thus no one really loses. Consensus does NOT mean that everyone feels that the final decision is the best possible alternative. It DOES mean that everyone believes they can, and will agree to, "live with" the decision even though they might have preferred something else.

Consensus

We find that the consensus model has many advantages over other models whenever constraints permit it to be used. For one thing, people affected by the decision are much more likely to "buy-in" to the decision when they've been involved in the process. Consensus is a concept which permeates all levels of the Simple Cooperation model. It reflects the fundamental premise that each member of the group must be respected, and encouraged to participate in all activities to the maximum of his/her capacity.

Although we clearly tend to prefer the consensus model, here are some examples of times when the various other models might be appropriate:

Appropriate use of models

Figure 6.1 PROBLEM SOLVING

Part 1: SAMPLE BRAINSTORMED IDEAS vs CONSTRAINTS CHART

	CONSTRAINTS:		COMMENTS:
BRAINSTORMED IDEAS i.e. possible solutions:			

NOTES: This example is to demonstrate comparing brainstromed ideas to constraints. The problem is identified and written on the chalk board or chart paper. Since the entire class is involved, consensus has been selected as the decision making model.

PROBLEM: What to do for year end party?
DECISION MAKING MODEL: Consensus
DECISION MAKER: Whole class

The next step is to identify the **CONSTRAINTS.** School rules, teacher judgement and cost are all considerations. In this example we are assuming that school transportation is not possible, thus one constraint is that the location of the activity must be within **WALKING DISTANCE** of the school. Secondly, based on her/his familiarity with the students and their families, the teacher has specified a maximum cost of $3.00 per student. Constraints are also written on the board.

Figure 6.2 PROBLEM SOLVING

Part 2:   SAMPLE BRAINSTORMED IDEAS vs CONSTRAINTS CHART

	CONSTRAINTS:		COMMENTS:
1. Go to zoo			
2. Go to beach			
3. Have potluck in classroom & play games			
4. Have picnic at park			
5. Go to Mary's house for Bar-B-Que			
6. Have film festival in classroom; eat in cafeteria			
7. Go to MacDonald's			

NOTES: Students have been given 4 minutes to brainstorm ideas. All student ideas have been listed on the form. The next step is to add the contraints and compare the ideas to the constraints.

Figure 6.3 **PROBLEM SOLVING**

- -

Part 3:   SAMPLE BRAINSTORMED IDEAS vs CONSTRAINTS CHART

- -

	CONSTRAINTS:		**COMMENTS:**
	Within walking distance	Cost: Maximum $3.00 per	
1. Go to zoo		X	need bus
2. Go to beach		X	need bus
3. Have potluck in classroom & play games	X	X	
4. Have picnic at park	X	X	
5. Go to Mary's house for Bar-B-Que	X	X	
6. Have film festival in classroom; eat in cafeteria	X	X	are films available?
7. Go to MacDonald's	X	X	

NOTES: The comparison chart is now completed. For demonstration purposes, we have identified the park, Mary's house and MacDonald's as being within walking distance of the school.

We now have 4 or 5 options depending upon the availability of films. The NEXT STEP is to discuss the advantages and disadvantages of each option. The class then identifies the preferred activities. Usually the list will be reduced to 1-3 choices.

The easiest thing to do at this point is to take each possibility separately and ask each student if they would feel OK if "this one" were selected. The option that ALL students feel okay about is the one selected.

— The teacher uses the AUTOCRATIC model when establishing the initial classroom standards, and when designing the lesson plan.

— The DEMOCRATIC model would be a good one to use when a group is deciding between two equally appealing activities or when time is short and no one in the group is going to feel they will lose something valuable to them.

— The PARTICIPATORY model can be valuable in any number of classroom situations in which the teacher must be the ultimate decision maker, but in which suggestions from the group can be considered and would be helpful; in choosing, for example, among possible destinations for a class outing.

SUMMARY OF KEY POINTS

• Cohesive groups do not occur by accident.

• Stages of group development include: teacher setting standards, getting acquainted, students setting standards, completing the task, and breaking-up.

• Conflict is inherent in the group development process.

• Conflict is best handled using a problem solving mode.

• Problem solving includes several specific steps: identifying the problem, identifying the ultimate decision maker, determining the decision making model to be used, specifying constraints relative to the solution, brainstorming possible solutions, comparing the brainstormed ideas to the list of constraints, selecting and implementing the solution, and evaluating the results.

• Four models of decision making included in Simple Cooperation are: autocratic, democratic, participatory, and consensus.

• Consensus decision making means that everyone can "live with" the selected decision even though it may not be their preferred action.

• While Simple Cooperation is based on consensus decision making, each of the four models is appropriate at specific times.

CHAPTER 4
GROUP ROLES AND MEETING MANAGEMENT

OVERVIEW

This chapter discusses the six major group roles and how to teach them. Delineation and assignment of the group roles is a critical element in effective group process.

Group roles are also an integral aspect of meeting management. Although we do not usually think of the classroom as a meeting, it is indeed a meeting as are smaller cooperative groups. Once we adjust our thinking, we can easily see the value of initiating effective meeting management strategies in the classroom.

A meeting occurs anytime two or more people come together or assemble for a specific purpose. Since the class has a single broad purpose — that of maximizing the potential of each of its members — it can and should be considered to be a meeting. When the class is subdivided into smaller cooperative groups, with their own specific purposes, these groups are in a meeting when they are working together. There are obviously differences in the structure and content between a meeting of, say, a community advisory group or a school board and a classroom meeting. However, all groups are based on member roles and responsibilities; and all groups, large or small, will be more apt to accomplish their goals if they operate within a structure — a structure that assures that all members have an equal chance to participate and succeed. Each student in the group needs to feel important and valued and that she/he has an equal chance to experience responsibilities of the various group roles. This is true of all meetings and it is critical within the Simple Cooperation model.

Meetings

Member roles and responsibilities

We will be describing the group roles within the Simple Cooperation class in some depth, and showing how these roles can be taught. Each Simple Cooperation group has a number of roles (see Figure 7) that will be new to the students, and to most of you as teachers. As you will see, each of these roles plays an important part in the whole group's functioning. They also teach specific skills to the individual students as they learn each role. These

Roles play an important part in the group's functioning

Figure 7

COOPERATIVE GROUP ROLES					— — — — —group size = 2-6

GROUP MEMBER	PRAISER	FACILITATOR as MONITOR	TIME-KEEPER	RECORDER: SINGLE ASSIGNMENT
on time; attends to task; shares ideas; contributes to product;	compliments group & individuals for staying on task, and other identified behaviors	gets: assignments from teacher; other resources necessary for group to complete assignment	tells group how much time is left for assignment; gives 5 & 10 minute warnings	writes/records group answers

CHECKER	OBSERVER	RECORDER: BRAINSTORM PROBLEM SOLVING	STUDENT FACILITATOR
has answer key — checks accuracy of individual and group responses	counts frequency of specific behaviors	writes/records group work, ideas, decisions	helps group achieve goals; suggests processes to be used

roles do not occur spontaneously. Each must be introduced, explained to the class, and modeled by the teacher. Just one new role is introduced at a time, modeled, and practiced until it is mastered before moving on to the next new role.

Some roles, Recorder and Facilitator for instance, are taught first at a simple level, then later are reintroduced at a more advanced level. A suggested sequence for teaching group roles will be found in Figure 8 to help clarify the order of introduction and guide you in choosing a sequence suitable for your own class.

Introduction of roles

THE "MEMBER"

The member

Students (and even some teachers) may assume that they already know what a GROUP MEMBER's role is...it's someone who attends a meeting, period. This is emphatically NOT true. The members of any group have very definite responsibilities. The teacher must first point out that the group can't do its task as well unless all members do their parts — everyone is equally important and valuable.

The teacher should discuss with the entire class the responsibilities of the group member's role as outlined below, and their importance to the group's success. Remember: regardless of other roles he/she may take, EACH STUDENT IS ALWAYS A GROUP MEMBER and as such is always responsible:

Responsibilities of the member

— to arrive at the meeting (classroom, area in the classroom) punctually. Tardiness breaks the flow of work already started.

— to participate actively, contribute ideas, give feedback. It isn't fair to anyone, including oneself, if a group member doesn't contribute her/his ideas to the group's task and product.

— to attend to the task and refrain from distracting the group by being off-task. Time is wasted and quality of work lowered unless every member gives undivided attention to the task at hand.

— to help the group complete its assignment. Members are collectively and individually responsible for the completion of the assignment. Also, the members' grades are dependent

Figure 8: GROUP ROLES CONTINUUM

1. GROUP MEMBER
2. PRAISER
3. FACILITATOR AS MONITOR
4. RECORDER: SINGLE ASSIGNMENT
5. TIME-KEEPER
6. CHECKER
7. OBSERVER
8. RECORDER: BRAINSTORMING, PROBLEM SOLVING
9. STUDENT FACILITATOR

upon everyone working together towards a common goal.

— to follow through on assignments or agreements. This is asking to keeping one's word. The group depends on each member doing what she/he has agreed to do. It hurts everyone (and the group grade) when one person doesn't fulfill his/her agreement.

— to listen to the other members of the group. Every member is important and has ideas to contribute.

— to take turns speaking: a skill that relates directly to listening. No one person should monopolize the entire discussion. Everyone must be given the chance to voice their thoughts, ideas, reactions.

— to encourage the other members of the group. Members should ask for each other's opinions and ideas, and compliment each other for a job well done, a good suggestion, or other good participation.

THE "PRAISER"

The praiser

The praiser's job is to give compliments and praise to members of the group or to the whole group for specific pre-selected behaviors: staying on task, completing assignments, returning quietly after a break, etc.

Students typically don't know how to give and receive compliments or praise, yet this social skill is extremely important. (Consider your feelings about the employer or administrator who knows how to praise as opposed to the one who doesn't, who never seems to notice a job well done.) Praising gracefully and sincerely is a high art. So is accepting praise or compliments: we all know people who just can't handle praise, no matter how sincere.

Because most students are so unfamiliar with praising, it's important to have an initial discussion with them about these skills. At elementary levels (K-6) you might begin by asking the class to define "praise" or "compliment." Ask students how they feel when giving a compliment or getting one. Then ask for examples of praise or a compliment, and ask how the receiver

Introducing praising to the class

might respond.

With older students you might begin this discussion by asking how people usually react when praised or complimented; by blushing, or brushing the compliment aside? (which, by the way, is a put-down because it rejects or contradicts the praiser's comment.) Ask for volunteers to describe how they feel when they're complimented/praised — embarrassed? on the spot? singled out? uncomfortable? Ask the students for suggestions about how to receive a compliment or praise. If they don't seem to know, tell them that a simple "Thank you" is fine, and including the praiser's name is even better: "Thank you, David." Longer responses are good, too, as long as they don't include a denial or put-down: "Thank you, David. I'm glad I could help." *Older students*

It might be helpful to have a brief discussion on the reasons that some of us are embarrassed and uncomfortable when praised. These might include: being taught that nobody is better than anybody else, that humility is virtuous, that it isn't nice to be the center of attention.

After these initial discussions, you can appoint a Praiser for a specific part of a class day. (Once this role is mastered, the role of Praiser is rotated among the students, usually on a daily basis.) Assign the Praiser a single behavior to watch for and praise or compliment, at a level appropriate to the age of the students

You may want to assign praising roles during whole class activities when first beginning. This will provide you an opportunity to monitor and support praising behavior. Later, after ample practice, praising may then be introduced into Simple Cooperation group activities. (At the end of this discussion you will find a list of behaviors that might be targeted for praise, and you will think of many others appropriate for your class.) Tell the class which behaviors the Praiser will be watching for during the time assigned. This will heighten students' awareness and place the target behavior at the forefront of everyone's attention. Throughout the time period, the Praiser should watch for students who deserve praise and give it to them quietly and simply. The Praiser might simply say: "Good job of staying on task." or "You're really paying attention. That's great." The student would accept *Heighten students' awareness* the compliment/praise just as simply. Note that the Praiser remains an active member of the group and participates in task completion.

As students master this skill, you can expand the list of behaviors to be praised in a given period, up to the limit of the Praiser's ability to keep track of them.

Mastery

You may be surprised to find how difficult it is for students to learn the role of Praiser, and to respond graciously to compliments and praise. Here are some additional activities and strategies you might find helpful:

— Practice giving and receiving compliments. The teacher can model: "Mellissa, I really liked the way you came in the room and got right to work today." "Jenna, I really appreciated the way you helped me with the door this morning." Whatever examples are used, they must be specific and sincere.

Giving and receiving compliments

Initially some of the students may go overboard, and it will all seem phoney and insincere. At first, the students may only be able to praise at a very superficial level, particularly at younger ages: "I like you hair/I like your dress/Your shirt is pretty." With time and practice you will see students becoming more sincere and perceptive.

— Give an optional assignment to praise or compliment three other people during the day. Make it clear that this is not a mandatory assignment. Tell class members that you would like them to try, but if they don't that's alright. If the optional assignment is given, it's important to follow up at the end of the day by asking volunteers how they felt giving compliments, and how the other person received them.

SAMPLE LIST OF BEHAVIORS FOR PRAISING

Sample list

— arriving at work area promptly
— being on task
— asking questions
— perception checking
— sharing ideas

— initiating discussion
— providing additional resources for group to complete task
— volunteering to do something related to group goal
— helping others

THE "FACILITATOR" AS MONITOR

At younger ages the role of Facilitator is much the same as the traditional Monitor role. With older students the role of Facilitator will become more complex, as we'll discuss later. We recommend introducing the role and using the term "Facilitator" even at this early level, to accustom the students to the concepts and responsibilities they will later expand to a full Facilitator role. In grades K-5, the Facilitator as Monitor role includes:

Facilitator as monitor

— getting and distributing worksheets, written assignments, etc., for all group members. Either the student Facilitator goes to the teacher's location for the papers/packets, or the teacher goes from group to group giving them to the Facilitator in each one, using the word "Facilitator" to build familiarity with the concept.

Responsibilities

— getting other materials necessary for completing the assignment. For example, if the group needs a dictionary, the Facilitator would go to the shelves and get it.

— collecting group work to turn in to the teacher, either turning it in to the teacher's location or giving it to the teacher as she he circulates among the groups. The student Facilitator should be reminded to avoid disturbing or distracting other groups when she/he is moving about the room. The Facilitator must make no unnecessary noise, stop to chat with others, or dawdle along the way.

THE "RECORDER" — SINGLE ASSIGNMENT

The Recorder keeps a record of the group's discussion or answers. This role is introduced first in a simple form, when the group is working on a lesson which will produce a single answer sheet. We'll introduce this role again later, at a more sophisticated level, for use when the group is working on brainstorming or problem solving assignments.

Recorder — single assignment

Besides giving the group an on-going record of its activities, the role of Recorder helps train students to listen attentively and selectively, to condense ideas in short note-form, and to make clear, legible records. This role, too, should be rotated among the students, so that all have a chance to learn these skills.

In a single-answer lesson, each member of the group is provided with individual worksheets. Each student contributes to the responses, then the Recorder prepares the final answer sheet to turn in to the teacher. All group members should sign the answer sheet indicating their agreement with the final product.

Responsibilities

THE "TIME-KEEPER"

The role of Time-keeper is relatively simple, but important to the functioning of the group. The Time-keeper helps the group pace itself by keeping track of how much time has been used at a task. This role can be combined with the Observer role or assigned separately.

Time-keeper

Teaching the Time-keeper role is simply a matter of explaining the responsibilities of the role:

Responsibilities

1) to tell the group periodically how much time has been spent on the task/assignment and how much time is left. If an hour has been allocated to writing a paper describing a recent news event, at the end of 30 minutes the Time-keeper would say something like: "We have used 30 minutes and we have 30 minutes left."

2) to give 10 and 5 minute warnings before the expiration of the time.

3) to advise the group when its time is up.

THE "CHECKER"

This role is appropriate when a group of students is studying for tests such as spelling or math, in which answers are either right or wrong. The Checker has the answer key and tells the members of the group whether their answers are right or wrong. (The Checker usually doesn't give a right answer, but may if the teacher feels this would be useful.)

The checker

Responsibilities

For example, when a cooperative group is studying for a spelling test, a list of the spelling words is given to the Checker. Going clockwise around the group, the Checker asks the person on her/his immediate right to spell the word "hypothetical." The student says, "H I G H P O T H E T I C A L." The Checker replies simply "No" or "Wrong" and the next person to the right is asked to spell the word. When the first person spells the word properly, the Checker says "Right" or "Correct" and gives a new word to the next student in line. Some variations of the Checker role are offered in the lesson activities found in Section II.

THE "OBSERVER"

Like the Praiser, the role of Observer is to provide feedback — but of a very different kind.

The observer

Both watch specific behaviors of the group or individual members and respond to them. But while the Praiser's response is specifically evaluative or judgmental, the Observer's response is strictly quantitative, with NO evaluation or judgment content. The Observer's role is descriptive only. Its purpose is to improve group interaction and increase the efficiency and effectiveness of the group by giving objective feedback about how often a desired behavior is actually occurring.

The Observer is assigned a specific behavior to observe. She/he does not actively participate in the group activity, but sits just outside the group in a position that allows her/him to see each member. Using a simple form, the Observer counts and records the frequency of the specific target behavior. (Figures 9.1 and 9.2 display sample Observation forms.) At the end of the time period, the Observer reports back to the group.

Responsibilities

A key to understanding the Observer role is teaching what a "behavior" is. A behavior is something that can be seen or heard. A behavior is something that can be COUNTED, i.e. it is quantifiable. A behavior is not an attitude, value, feeling, judgment or evaluation. "John is rude" is not a behavior, it is a judgment. It doesn't tell anything about John, it only tells how the speaker FEELS about him. "John interrupted Cindy three times in the last ten minutes" is a behavior. It can be counted, and it gives

Key to understanding the observer role

solid information. "John is rude" is an evaluation and can only result in bad feelings. "John interrupted Cindy three times" gives John information that can help him change his behavior.

To teach this difference it's helpful to write two columns on the chalkboard. In one column generate a list of behaviors from the students, both positive and negative. In the other column generate a list of feelings, values and/or judgments that might be confused with a behavior. In the behavior list might be words such as: interrupt, make noise, come late to class, praise, offer ideas. In the Feelings list might be: rude, distracting, nice, mean, pretty. If a student offers a judgment word for the Behavior list, simply ask if it can be counted, and without further comment write it in the Feeling column. (Remember, students shouldn't be embarrassed nor made to feel that they are dumb for making a mistake.)

You will have a chance to bring up another critical point during this activity: the feelings associated with behaviors are subjective. Behaviors seen as rude to one person may seem polite to another, depending upon a variety of factors. Remember, for example, the question of eye contact between children and adults, which is seen as impolite in some cultures and polite in others.

Instruction

The next step is to give instruction on how to observe. An Observation form is used (refer back to Figures 9.1 and 9.2) which lists behavior(s) to be observed and the group members' names. Let's use "Praising" as an example of a target behavior. You've taught this concept and practiced it until you feel the group is ready for a formal observation. You may want to take the role of Observer for yourself, the first time or two. After informing the group that you will be observing praising behavior during the next activity or time period, seat yourself to one side and count praising as it occurs. At the end of the time, report back to the students without editorializing: Michael praised 3 times, Suzanne praised 4 times, David praised 2 times, Mike praised no time, Cindy praised 8 times. (Editorializing includes such subtle cues as: "Suzanne praised 4 times, David only praised 2 times." The interjection of "only" connotes an evaluation — it is a qualifier.)

Responsibilities

Figure 9.1

SAMPLE OBSERVATION FORM (PRIMARY)

Praise
Praise
Praise

Make a check mark (✓) each time someone
in the group PRAISES another person.

Jessica

Blackie

Sylvia

Smokey

Figure 9.2

SAMPLE OBSERVATION FORM	NAMES:				
Praising					
Having eye contact with speaker/listener					
Clarifying by asking questions					
Clarifying by paraphrasing					
Summarizing what has been said					
Owning own feelings/opinions					
Encouraging others					
Helping to keep group on task					
Sharing ideas					
Perception checking, e.g. asking others how they feel about progress and process					
Initiating discussion					
Identifying feelings by name					
Providing additional resources for group to complete task					
Volunteering to do something related to group goal					

NOTES: This is for demonstration purposes only. You would list 1-6 behaviors to be observed (the number being dependent upon the student's skill level).

The Observer's feedback will help the students and their group to see how often or seldom they're doing the desired behavior. It recognizes and reinforces the behavior without condemning the lack of it with judgments and evaluations.

Here are some other activities and points to remember about the Observer role:

— Observation may be of a group behavior or individual behavior. The Observer may record how many times the group collectively demonstrated the behavior without naming individuals or how many times names individual members did the behavior.

— Primary-age children can be taught to observe even if they can't read or write. Symbols or pictures can identify the behavior; a smiley face, a cartoon of someone with their hands to their ears because of noise, etc. Color codes can be used instead of names, with each student wearing a colored tag that matches a space on the observation form.

— At any grade level, it's important to teach, practice and observe one behavior at a time and to be sure of mastery before adding another. At the secondary level it's possible to observe as many as 10 or 20 behaviors by the end of the school year, while primary students may master just one.

Mastery

When students are observing each other we suggest observation of positive behaviors such as praising and contributing to the discussion. Positive based observations enhance the supportive atmosphere in the classroom.

THE "RECORDER": BRAINSTORMING, PROBLEM SOLVING

Earlier we introduced the Recorder role at a simple level. As the group matures, and with older students, you can teach a more complex level of the Recorder role. This role's primary use is in brainstorming and problem solving, though it can also be used in other group activities in which it's important to keep track of what's being said in group discussion. The recorder usually does

Recorder: brainstorming, problem solving

not take part in the group activity, but concentrates on the Recording role.

It's best if the Recorder uses a large sheet of paper hung on the wall — or, if no wall space is available, on a chart stand or even on the floor. The Recorder writes key words and phrases from critical elements of the group discussion and records any decisions made.

Responsibilities

The Recorder doesn't write down every single word; rather, he/she writes key words from a speaker's longer statement. For example, if the group's task is to plan a study unit on local history, and decides that one activity will be to take a walking tour of historical sites in the town/neighborhood, the Recorder should NOT write "See old houses and buildings," but rather "Walking tour of historical sites."

The role of Recorder helps students learn to write neatly, since the notes she/he takes are important to the group task and group members will tell the recorder if they can't read the notes. It trains the students to listen closely and selectively, to be able to identify and pull out key words from a long statement. However, if the group is going too fast for the Recorder, he/she should certainly ask group members to slow down or wait a moment until the record can be brought up to date.

Recording is a skill that must be modeled and practiced extensively before the teacher can expect mastery of it. As students become more skilled in the role of Recorder, and at high school or adult levels, other techniques may be added:

Must be modeled and practiced

— Different colors may be used for each major point of a discussion, and yellow or orange used to highlight critical points or decisions.

— Abbreviations and symbols, such as +, =, (,), may be used, instead of words, to identify or note certain concepts or actions, and to help recording go more quickly.

THE "STUDENT FACILITATOR"

This is the most difficult role to master in its purest form.

Student facilitator

Earlier we described the Facilitator-Monitor role, as a preparation for this more advanced level of facilitation. To be able to handle this role, students should already have achieved a relatively high level of communication skills such as paraphrasing and perception checking. (All of the other group roles will have helped prepare students for the Facilitator role, too: praising, observing, recording, time-keeping.)

The responsibilities of the Facilitator are: *Responsibilities*

> — to define the responsibilities of the group, making sure the group's purpose is clearly understood by all members.

> — to focus on group PROCESS not PRODUCT. The Facilitator is concerned with how the group is working, not the specific content of the discussion.

> — to encourage all members to participate, to contribute ideas, opinions, suggestions.

> — to make sure that all members have a chance to speak; that the discussion isn't monopolized by one or a few members.

> — to help the group reach its goal and objectives by suggesting processes to be used. The Facilitator might suggest polling the group, breaking into smaller groups with sub-tasks, brainstorming, stopping general discussion to go round the circle sharing ideas individually.

> — to call time-out if the group seems to be stalled, perhaps suggesting a break and giving a time at which to reconvene.

> — to keep the group on task, calling it back if it has wandered off-task and gotten involved in side-issues.

> — to help the group agree on a decision making model if decisions are to be made, and to ensure that all members agree on the model to be used.

> — to keep the group within the time parameters of the task, help it pace itself along the various stages of the process in order to complete the task on time.

The facilitator usually does not participate in the group activities at the same time she/he is filling this role. Clearly this role requires extensive practice, and must be modeled thoroughly by the teacher.

REMEMBER TO ROTATE THE ROLE AMONG MEMBERS OF THE GROUP SO ALL HAVE A CHANCE TO PRACTICE THESE SKILLS.

SUMMARY OF KEY POINTS

• The classroom as a whole, as well as smaller Simple Cooperation groups, should be viewed as meetings.

• Group Roles are a critical element in the Simple Cooperation model.

• Specific Group Roles include: Group Member, Praiser, Time-Keeper, Recorder for single assignments, Facilitator as monitor, Recorder for Brainstorming and Problem Solving, Observer, and Student Facilitator.

• Responsibilities for each role were discussed in detail.

• A Group Roles continuum was provided as a guide in sequencing the teaching of each role.

CHAPTER 5
SELECTING STUDENT GROUPS

OVERVIEW
Student groups may be homogeneous or heterogeneous, teacher-selected or student-selected. Whatever method is used, the formation of Simple Cooperation groups must be done in a careful and considered manner. Your lesson objective, subject area content, student ability level and student personalities are the bases for determining which students will work together as a group.

This chapter discusses a variety of methods for group selection and the rationale for using each method.

Since a central thrust of the Simple Cooperation method is to teach students how to function well in groups, you will need to learn techniques for selecting students to work together in combinations. The classroom group as a whole is a given. Smaller cooperative groups will be formed constantly throughout the school year. Their formation MUST be done consciously. Each lesson lends itself to specific grouping decisions. You must choose a grouping pattern that is a "best fit" for each lesson, and use a selection method that suits the needs of the students and the atmosphere of the classroom at the time.

Group formation

Groups may be large or small, homogenous or heterogeneous, short or long term, have academic or student social tasks, be teacher or self-selected, be formed by random or structured selection methods. Whatever their makeup or method of selection, the things to remember when forming a Simple Cooperation group are:

Things to remember

— Introduce just one new role at a time, and model and practice it until students have thoroughly mastered the new role. The number of roles being used in any one group depends on how many have been taught and mastered, and what's appropriate/necessary for the lesson at hand.

— Have an objective for grouping clearly in mind: know what you are trying to achieve.

— Describe to the students the group selection method that will be used.

— Model the selection procedure, if needed.

— Always check for understanding. Make sure the students understand which group they are to join or the planned activity for group selection, where they will be working, etc., before starting the group formation process.

— If your first few attempts at group selection aren't as successful as you would like, don't despair! Talk with the class about what went wrong and what worked, then give it another try. Remember that all of you are learning, teacher as well as students, and learning takes time and practice.

We'll discuss some of the issues involved in group selection and formation, and then give you several methods for forming groups in the classroom.

Duration of group

A group may be together as briefly as three minutes (for an opening activity, for instance,) or as long as six weeks (a communication or a long term academic group.) Once a group is formed it should stay together for the entire length of the project. Students must get a clear message that they will be together until the task is completed. They will be working through their group development process, and this may well include conflict. If conflict does erupt, don't immediately resort to removing a student from the group in order to resolve it. Remember that conflict should not be regarded as a negative. The students need to learn ways to turn conflict into problem solving and communication challenges. Only a serious and irremedial threat to the group's function should lead to removal of a group member, since removing a member gives the message that you don't really expect the students to be able to resolve the situation.

Rule of thumb

As a rule of thumb, the less skilled the students are in group management and communication techniques, the smaller the group should be. As these skills improve, group sizes can be increased. (See the end of this section for an age and group level chart.) In larger groups there are more people interacting, listening, speaking, clarifying and making decisions. Students in large groups must be able to wait their turn to speak, and must know when it's appropriate to make comments or suggest ideas.

It takes a fair degree of sophistication, patience and skill to do this well, and students will have to work up to it gradually. Remember that each stage of development must be mastered thoroughly before moving on to the next.

Recommended group size by grade level is:

Recommended group size

GRADE LEVEL		GROUP SIZE
Pre-school	=	*2*
Kindergarten	=	2 - 3
Grade 1	=	2 - 3
Grades 2 & 3	=	2 - 4
Grades 4 & 5	=	2 - 5
Grades 6 - adult	=	2 - 6

ACADEMIC GROUPS

Academic groups are normally scheduled for 1-6 weeks. The academic group may have a single, specific objective (practicing for a spelling test, completing a social studies report, etc.) or it may have a multi-objective assignment (several members drawing a pictorial sequence of the War of 1812, while several others are writing the captions.) It may be made up of students with similar skills and aptitudes (homogeneous) or be a mix of skill levels (heterogeneous).

Academic groups

Homogeneous groups may be assigned a single, specific objective which is appropriate to the group members' abilities. It is important to recognize here that there is really no such thing as homogeneity — we can never group students on exactly the same level, for within each group will be a combination of specific strengths and weaknesses. Look at this as an asset, not a liability, for the shared thinking skills will bring strength to the group. Homogeneous grouping is appropriate for such activities as study groups, completion of worksheets, and in fact, any other task that is normally assigned an individual student.

Homogeneous groups

In a heterogeneous academic group, the assignment might include two (or more) objectives within the group's overall lesson assignment. For example, if the group is working on capitalization, two objectives might be: 1) capitalizing the first word in a sentence, and 2) capitalizing proper names.

Heterogeneous groups

Given 10 sentences on a group worksheet, specific students are assigned to each of the objectives. Set a time limit for the lesson. Tell the students that they will work individually for a specified part of the time, then discuss each answer until they agree on it. If the role of Time-keeper has been taught, one may be assigned; if not, you should act as Time-keeper to signal when the group begins discussion, and give 10 and 5 minute warnings before the end of the allocated time.

As we discussed in the first chapter, the heterogeneous group benefits students on all skill levels, by providing for sharing of thinking skills. The Simple Cooperation model, as evidenced in its very name, involves students working cooperatively together, so that the skills and experience of the individual students can become the skills and experiences of all.

Sharing of thinking skills

METHODS OF TEACHER GROUP SELECTION

— NAME TAGS

Teacher selection—

Name tags

For either heterogeneous or homogeneous groups this method lets you form groups carefully, without calling unwanted attention to the principles behind the selection — academic levels, social skills, etc.

Choose an identifying number, letter, or name for each group and a workspace for each. Write a tag (or a sign) to identify each group and put it at that group's workspace. Write each student's name on a tag and lay the tags out in the groups you are forming. This will help you visualize the groups. Just like a hostess working out seating arrangements, you can shuffle the tags around until you have a grouping that seems to work best. When you've decided on each group, write that group's identifying symbol on the student members' tags.

Give each student the tag with her/his name on it and tell the class that everyone should find the workspace or table with a symbol (letter, name, etc.) that matches the one on his/her own tag and gather there.

For pre-school and early elementary students you might want to use color codes, pictures, or other symbols on the tags instead of names. You could also use paper hats made by you or the students.

— WALL CHARTS

Wall charts

Homogeneous or heterogeneous groups of students preselected by you are written on a chart and posted on the wall before the lesson. (A sample wall chart is reflected in Figure 10.)

If time permits, you may wish to have the students choose the group name as their first group task or assignment.

— MYSTERY ENVELOPES

Mystery envelopes

For pre-determined grouping write the name of each student on an envelope. As in the NAME TAG method, sort the envelopes into groups until the formation looks right to you. Choose a selection of small objects for each group and put the objects in each envelope for that group. One group, for instance, might have a pencil and a paper clip in each member's envelope, and another might have an eraser and a piece of chalk in each member's envelope. Seal and distribute the envelopes to the students.

Tell the students to feel the contents of the envelopes. (They might want to guess what the objects are, but that's not the primary task.) Tell them they aren't to open their Mystery Envelopes yet, but only to feel the contents until they're thoroughly familiar with the number and shapes of the objects.

Next, tell the students how many others in the room have envelopes with the same contents. If you've prepared for groups of three, for instance, say: "Two other people have envelopes that are exactly like yours. Your task is to find them. When you do, choose your working space and be seated with your new group."

Figure 10

SAMPLE WALL CHART

GROUP 1	GROUP 2	GROUP 3	GROUP 4
NAME: Sluggers	NAME: Willit's Wonders	NAME: Chino's Greats	NAME: Sunny Sides
Jenna	Mellissa	Cleo	David
Cindy	Suzanne	Clarence	Margaret
Mike	Micheal	Tom	Bill

GROUP 5	GROUP 6	GROUP 7	GROUP 8
NAME: Orlando Tigers	NAME: Lions	NAME: Dolphins	NAME: Surfers
Billy	Robert	Jason	Virginia
Kathy	Anthony	Pat	Tommy
Billie Jo	Gregory	Heath	Dawn

Lastly, direct the students to open their envelopes and check their accuracy.

METHODS OF RANDOM GROUP SELECTION

Random selection

Random selection of groups is appropriate for non-academic activities or academic activities in which careful articulation of student ability levels isn't essential.

— MYSTERY ENVELOPES

Mystery envelopes

The same as described in **METHODS OF TEACHER GROUP SELECTION**, only without student names on the envelopes. Distribute envelopes at random and proceed as explained. This will be slightly more chaotic, of course.

— COUNTING OFF

Counting off

Decide how many groups will be formed and give each a number. Then assign a corresponding number to each child. For example, if there are four groups, tell each student, in turn, that they are a 1, 2, 3, or 4. Alternatively, the students may count themselves off. For this, indicate one student to begin and what sequence to use — around the room, up and down the rows, etc.

You may place numbered signs or tags at selected workspaces in the room and tell the students to cluster at the number which matches theirs, or simply tell each group where to meet.

— SELF GROUPING BY CATEGORY

Self grouping by category

Sometimes a bit of controlled chaos is a welcome breather. This method is a good one for such times. It also gives the students an element of choice in forming groups, while insuring a good "mix-up." (This is a good method for "getting acquainted" times, too — choose categories that help the students learn about each other: who rides the school bus, who has a baby in their home, who has a sister, etc.)

Tell the students to sort themselves into groups of 4, or whatever size group you want to form. Tell them that each group must have at least one member who represents one of a list of categories: for example, 1) someone wearing shoes with laces, 2) someone with brown hair, 3) someone wearing blue, and 4) someone who was born out of state. Tell them it's "OK" to have a person who fits more than one of the categories, but that each group must have all categories represented.

The groups are then directed to their workplaces and are seated.

— LINE FORMATION

Line formation

Instruct the students to form themselves into a line. When this is done, count off down the line in groups of whatever size you've determined is needed. For example, for groups of three, you would say to the students at the beginning of the line: "1, 2, 3, —you're the first group. I'd like you to sit at the table by the door." After the students have been seated, continue the process until all students have been grouped and seated.

— THE BIRTHDAY LINE

The birthday line

(This group selection method was developed by Dr. Stanley Schainker from San Francisco and is used with permission.)

Have students arrange themselves according to the month and date of their birthdays. Ask who was born in January, and help the January group "discover" who has the earliest birthdate. Tell this student that she/he is first in line, and direct him/her to stand at some appropriate place in the room. Then help the students in the December group discover who has the last birthday, and direct that student to stand at the end of the line. Have the other students then arrange themselves in a line between the identified students in the correct order.

— ALPHABET LINE

Alphabet line

Explain that students will arrange themselves in alphabetical order according to first or last names. (With some groups you might want to use name tags.) As in the Birthday Line, help the students "discover" who will be first and last in line and tell them where these two students will stand.

— THE COLOR SPECTRUM

The color spectrum

This is a good method to use when selecting groups for art projects. Begin by reviewing a color spectrum chart if there's one in the classroom. If not, you can write the names of colors on the chalkboard. You may want to check for understanding by having children point out an example of each color in the room. Then direct the students to group themselves according to the color of socks, shirts, or other clothing they're wearing that day. If students are wearing uniforms or a range of colors isn't represented, you might want to use colored tags instead.

— SUBJECT AREA SELECTION   *Subject area selection*

Best for projects for which you want a heterogeneous mix of students and where group size can vary somewhat, as, for example, in an art collage project in which each group will bring pictures to use in the collage which relate to a specific subject in it. In this example, you would designate areas around the room for each subject or element in the collage, then tell the students to go stand by the one they'd like to work with.

Be prepared, with this selection method, to have large groups that must be subdivided or to eliminate a subject area if no students are interested in working with it.

SUMMARY OF KEY POINTS

• Simple Cooperation groups are formed with careful consideration to your lesson objective, subject area content, student ability level and student personalities.

• Groups may be heterogeneous or homogeneous, teacher selected or student self-selected.

• Groups may be formed for academic and/or social skills objectives.

• Groups stay together for the length of the activity whether that be three minutes or six weeks.

• Group size should never exceed 6 students.

• 11 methods of forming groups were described.

SOURCES:

NAME TAGS: Jacquie and Peggy

WALL CHARTS: Adapted for Simple Cooperation by Peggy

and Jacquie. It seems that wall charts have been used forever in classrooms. Original source unknown.

MYSTERY ENVELOPES: This activity has been used by workshop leaders in many workshops attended by both Peggy and Jacquie. Original source unknown.

COUNTING OFF: Original source unknown.

SELF GROUPING BY CATEGORY: Original source unknown.

THE BIRTHDAY LINE: Developed by Dr. Stan Schainker — Associate Superintendent, San Francisco Unified School District, San Francisco, CA.

THE ALPHABET LINE: Adaptation by Peggy and Jacquie of Dr. Schainker's Birthday Line.

THE COLOR SPECTRUM: Jacquie

SUBJECT AREA SELECTION: Jacquie

CHAPTER 6
PUTTING IT ALL TOGETHER

OVERVIEW

In the preceding chapters, the basic components of Simple Cooperation; i.e. group development, effective communication, group roles and meeting management, conflict and problem solving, have all been described in detail.

This final chapter addresses the "how-tos" of designing a Simple Cooperation lesson. A lesson plan format with instructions, sample lesson plans, and suggestions for room arrangement are included.

In addition, reward/grading systems and two methods for monitoring student progress (teacher observation and wrap-up) in both social and academic skills are discussed.

When implementing new methods in the classroom a frequently asked question is, "Where do I begin?" For that reason we have included a suggested social skills continuum. It should be used as a reference and beginning point and modified to best serve you and your students.

We have discussed each of the component parts of Simple Cooperation — Now it's time to get to the "nitty-gritty" of lesson design. At this point you may be saying to yourself: "STOP! How do I know FOR SURE that students are learning the social skills? We've had a lot of practice throughout the years measuring whether our students have met academic objectives. But what kind of checks and balances are in the Simple Cooperation model that can assist me in determining if the social objectives have been met?"

"Nitty-gritty of lesson design

Mastery of objectives, whether they are social or academic, are equally important. The Simple Cooperation model provides two methods for the teacher to monitor the attainment of objectives: TEACHER OBSERVATION and WRAP UP ACTIVITIES.

Mastery of objectives

TEACHER OBSERVATION

Teacher observation

Teacher observation provides a systematic method of monitoring student behavior relative to academic and social objectives. It is also a workable vehicle for providing immediate feedback to the students.

It is suggested that a simple observation form be used, one that can be adjusted to meet your needs. A sample teacher observation form is provided in Figure 11. We have found that this basic form adjusts easily to a variety of observation requirements. The form can be duplicated and ready for use when needed.

Observations may be conducted by targeting behaviors of individual students, groups of students, or the class as a whole. We suggest that you vary the method of observation, as is appropriate for you, your students and the lesson objective.

Target behaviors

It is not necessary to conduct observations during each Simple Cooperation lesson. Observe when you feel that student behavior may be a bit "off target," or when you are not really sure if you have gotten the message across and would like some objective data to assist you in decisions regarding lesson adjustment, or when you know the students are right "on target" and want to give them some positive feedback.

Usually teacher observation information is not used to grade students. Informal feedback given to students regarding your observations will heighten their awareness of specific academic and/or social behaviors.

During the teacher observation process you will move from group to group while the students are working on their assignment. You will have a checklist of specific behaviors you have decided to observe. You may focus on group or individual objectives.

For instance, if 'praising' is the behavior to be observed, you may choose to do five minute observations of each group and count the number of times members of the group praised during that five minute period. It is important that you stand apart from the group you are observing and be as unobtrusive as possible.

In this instance feedback would be presented to the class at the end of the session, "During the observation period Group 1 praised 5 times, Group 2 praised 10 times," and so on. As in student

Feedback

observation no value judgement is made during the feedback period. A simple statement of the facts is all that is required to get the message across.

Another alternative is to observe individuals within each group. In this case, you would stand apart from the group and observe for a given period of time (teacher observations usually are 2-5 minutes in length). Individual names of group members would be written on the observation forms.

Following your observation, you would stop the group process or wait for a natural break in the group activity and report your observations to the group. Again, a simple statement of the facts is all that is important. We have found that the message "gets across" quite nicely without making further comment.

After the observation of the first group is completed, you would move on to the next group and repeat the process. You may not get to every group during one activity period. That's okay; however, it IS important to periodically observe all the groups, even if your observations are spread out over a couple of activity periods of even over two days.

Remember that teacher observation is to assist you and your students to know whether or not specific skills have been mastered. (ONLY those skills that have been taught should be observed by the teacher.)

You may wish to refresh your memory on appropriate methods of giving feedback by referring to the student observation and feedback information found in Section I.

WRAP-UP

Wrap-up

The wrap-up is a very brief activity which occurs immediately after a Simple Cooperation lesson. Its primary purposes are to give each student the opportunity to think about his/her own cognitive and/or social behavior in a structured manner and to provide the teacher with immediate feedback regarding the process each group and/or individual is using and the learning that has occurred.

Simply put, you ask a question related to the academic lesson or

Integration of com-

Figure 11: SAMPLE TEACHER OBSERVATION FORM

STUDENT/GROUP NAMES:

Behaviors to be observed.						

the social skills involved in the group's process. Because wrap-up activities pose a question to students, they provide a natural integration of communication and thinking skills. Students must think about what has just occurred, what they have learned, how their group functioned and/or how they themselves behaved within the group. They must then communicate these thoughts to others.

munication and thinking skills

Wrap-up activities may be general or specific and related to the lesson's social or academic objective.

For example, a general academic question could be to name one new thing learned during the lesson. A more specific academic wrap-up question might be to identify the most critical element in whatever the lesson was about.

Academic wrap-up

A general social skill question may be to identify how the group worked together to complete the task. A more specific wrap-up would be to ask each student what she/he did to help the group complete the task.

Social skills wrap-up

There are numerous ways in which the wrap-up activity may be conducted such as: verbally within each Simple Cooperation group; verbally with the entire class; written and simply handed in to the teacher who then reads the responses to the class; or written on index cards, shuffled, then distributed to group or class members who then read them aloud.

DO NOT UNDERESTIMATE THE IMPORTANCE OF THE WRAP-UP ACTIVITY. Besides reinforcing academic content, thinking and communication skills, they bring closure to a lesson. Thus, students may begin to prepare themselves to move on to the next lesson or activity. They also provide valuable feedback to you, the teacher, which gives you ideas on how to adjust your lesson the next time.

Wrap-up is important

The most important factors to consider when planning wrap-up activities are:

Important factors

— The activity directly relates to the academic or social objective of the lesson.

— A wrap-up activity should immediately follow each Simple Cooperation lesson.

— The activity should take 3-10 minutes.

— The activity should be on the level of each student's abilities.

— The activity should not put anyone on the spot so that they feel embarrassed.

— The activity should vary in process — sometimes in small groups, sometimes pairs, and at other times with the class as a whole.

Sample wrap-up activities may be found in Section II.

ROOM ARRANGEMENT

Room arrangement

Another very important issue to consider before planning a Simple Cooperation lesson is room arrangement. Careful planning of desks, chairs, and students can assist you in designing a successful lesson.

Arrangements that we have found successful are:

— Clusters of movable desks.

— Small round or square tables.

— Sitting in circles on the floor.

In planning a room arrangement important factors to consider are:

— Students are facing each other. It is important that they are able to maintain eye contact and read nonverbal language.

— That you give clear directions about where each group is to work and/or post signs at the appropriate areas in the room.

— Physical movement of furniture is held to a minimum. Furniture movement can't be avoided but the rule of thumb is to keep it to a minimum.

GRADES AND REWARDS

The last issues we need to discuss before you design your first Simple Cooperation lesson is how to reward your students for cooperative work.

Grades and rewards, like cooperation, are not new to education. We grade our students every day. Most teachers also provide some sort of reinforcing rewards for student effort and achievement and many teachers provide full class rewards for specific behaviors or accomplishments.

You do not need to abolish your present grading or rewarding system to implement Simple Cooperation. Students will still be completing assignments individually, independent of any group. Thus, you will be grading that part of their work as you always have.

No need to abolish present system

What is different is giving a group grade or grading the individuals within a group based on the group product. Giving the same grade to each student in a small group may well be new to many teachers. This process frequently causes concern and worry to many. For that reason, we will spend the next few pages describing group grades and rewards.

What is different

GROUP GRADES

Group grades and rewards provide incentive and motivation to the student members of a Simple Cooperation group to "pull" together towards a mutual goal. Individual responsibility grows as each member of the group comes to the realization that the group will not succeed if he/she does not do his or her part of the assignment. For many students this will be the first time in their school career that they feel equally important and valuable as their classmates. As each student internalizes their importance, the quality of both the individual and group work will increase.

Mutual goal

Group grading simply means that every member of the group receives the very same grade for the assignment. For instance, if the assignment were an essay researching the causes of the Civil War and the group paper earned 85 points you, the teacher, would record 85 points for each member of that group. Ob-

Every group member receives same grade

viously, if one member of the group did not complete his or her part of the assignment the product would be of lesser quality and the group would receive a lower grade.

Note that in the above example each individual member of the group receives a grade which is recorded in the grade book next to that individual's name; however, that grade is based on the group product and EACH AND EVERY MEMBER OF THE GROUP RECEIVES THE SAME GRADE for that assignment. Individual members of a group are not given a grade that is different than their fellow-group members. The message must be clear that all members of the group are responsible for the group completing its assignment and that the individuals within the group will receive the same grade which is based on the quality and/or completion of the assigned task.

Grade is based on group product

All group members are responsible

Other examples of grading individuals within the group include:

• Group grade averaging: This method may be used when each individual group member is assigned a specific task. The group function is to assist its members to complete the assigned task and to check each other's work. As the teacher, you would grade each individual's work, average the group members' grades and give each member of the group the averaged grade. For instance, let's say that there are four group members whose grades are: 80, 75, 84 and 90. The average of those four grades is 82 which is the grade you would record for each of the four group members.

Group grade averaging

Variation: You could give two grades for the assignment — the individual's actual grade and the group average grade.

• Bonus points: When there is no grade for the assignment, a bonus point might be given to each member of the group for simply completing the assignment.

Bonus points

• Awards: Certificates, personal notes from the teacher, or other awards are given to each individual member of the group for completing the assignment or achieving a specified goal.

Awards

GROUP REWARDS

There will be many times that you will want to reward or grade groups as a whole unit. This procedure is especially appropriate for social skills objectives. For instance, if staying on task were the objective you could use a token or point system which could "buy" so much free time at the end of the week. In this case, you might offer groups five points for staying on task during a 15 minute assignment. If the entire group did, in fact, stay on task the GROUP would receive the five points. This means that EVERYONE in the group must stay on task and the group as a whole would earn the free time. Again, if one member of the group did not stay on task, the group would not earn the points.

Social skills

Group grades and rewards place the focus on the group as a whole meeting the objective (whether the objective relates to academic or social skills). With this focus, it becomes the ultimate responsibility of the group to ensure that all members participate and do their fair share.

Focus on the group

When first implementing Simple Cooperation there may well be times when groups do not complete the assignment. When this happens it is important for the group members to examine their behavior. They need to look at what went right and what went wrong in their group. Problem solving strategies and wrap-up sessions can aid this process.

These situations are part of the group growth process. Remember that students are not accustomed to being responsible to each other nor are they accustomed to being responsible for their own learning. The teacher acting as facilitator can greatly assist groups through these growth periods by monitoring individual and group behavior through the use of structured observations and providing non-evaluative feedback and suggestions.

Growth process

Teaching as facilitator

It is really tempting to use direct intervention strategies when conflicts or problems arise in groups. It is easy to remove a particularly argumentative or a non-participating student from a group. This is done in the belief that if we switch students from one group to another eventually we'll find an amiable mix. Usually, this does not solve the problem. In fact, it may be a disservice to the students and actually inhibit their learning. Direct teacher intervention gives the message to the group, and the class as a whole, that the teacher believes the group members are not capable of problem solving and finding a satisfactory

Direct intervention

Direct intervention gives messages to students

solution themselves. It conveys the message that the group can depend on the teacher to make certain that the group receives a good grade or reward. This type of direct intervention also tells students that they really do not have to be responsible for their own behavior or learning.

We are not saying that direct intervention should never occur —certainly there are crisis situations when you, the teacher, must intercede. We ARE saying that whenever possible it will help students more if you act as a facilitator and guide students through problem solving strategies when they encounter problems within their Simple Cooperation groups.

Rewards must be meaningful to the group as a whole as well as to the individual members of the group. For example, extra physical education time would not be a reward for the student who hates physical education or for the student with some type of physical limitation which prohibits her/him from participating in the activity. This "reward" could well be seen as a punishment by these children and they may covertly (or even overly) block the group's progress. Therefore, group rewards must be selected with care and consideration of the individual students comprising the group.

Rewards must be meaningful

While there are always some students who are rewarded simply by completing the task well, for many students a more tangible reward system is essential. An effective grading or reward system is very often the key to full group participation. This is especially true when first implementing Simple Cooperation in your classroom.

Tangible rewards are essential for some students

Some examples of group rewards are:

Examples of group rewards

• Bulletin Boards — Each group is listed on the bulletin board. Whenever the group completes the assigned task a sticker is placed after the group's name.

• Free Time — The group receives free time to play a game together. (May be earned immediately or by accumulating points over a few days.)

- Computer Center — The group is alloted a specific amount of time to work at the computer together, playing games or doing extra credit assignments. (As above, may be immediate or earned by accumulating points.)

- Edible Treats — The group would be given a healthy treat such as popcorn.

- Assignment Selection — The group would be given a choice of assignments or objectives for their next task.

- Extra Responsibility — The group would be in charge of distributing playground or physical education equipment.

- Helping the Teacher — Many young children like to help the teacher. If this is true in your class, a group reward could be to help the teacher erase the chalk board or take messages to the principal's office.

- Library Time — The group is provided extra library time.

In some cases, visiting the principal to show her/him their completed project would be an excellent group reward.

IMPORTANT POINTS TO REMEMBER
WHEN GIVING GROUP GRADES AND REWARDS

- Include some type of grade or reward for each lesson.

- Be clear and precise — Students should know exactly what they must do to receive the reward or grade. Provide a complete explanation before you begin the Simple Cooperation lesson. *Explain the grade or reward*

- Be consistent — Don't change the rules in midstream. Follow through on the reward or grading system that you established for the assignment. If it didn't work out quite the way you wanted, change the system NEXT time. *Follow through*

- Meaningful rewards — Make sure the reward is meaningful to the students involved. You may want to have the students help establish the reward system. For example, you could give the students a list of possible rewards and each group, using consensus decision making strategies, would select its own reward.

- Stay fresh — Vary the reward system to keep both you and your students motivated and interested.

• Reduce the frequency of extrinsic rewards — As time goes by many groups will become less dependent upon external rewards. When you notice this shift in motivation you might consider omitting a specific reward for certain assignments. This is really a matter of personal preference and teaching style. We know teachers who include some type of reward or grade for each and every assignment throughout the year, while others begin omitting an extrinsic reward as soon as possible.

DESIGNING A LESSON

Thus far we have discussed each of the component parts of Simple Cooperation. Four charts are presented to recap those parts: Figure 12 reflects the major components of Simple Cooperation; Figure 13 exhibits the various aspects of social skills; Figure 14 represents the area of academic skills; and Figure 15 displays lesson design.

Designing a lesson

Now let's review several important factors to remember when designing your lesson:

Important factors

— When planning academic activities, group membership should not be left to chance.

Group membership

— Academic objectives should be appropriate for each member of the group.

Academic objectives

— Lesson objectives should be clear to both the teacher and the students. It's a good idea to check the student's understanding of the lesson's objective and what they are to do. This can be done in many ways. For example:

Check for understanding

— You can ask a volunteer to paraphrase your instructions.

— When moving from group to group during a Simple Cooperation lesson, you can ask a member of each group: "What is the objective for this lesson." or "What are you supposed to do today?".

— Make sure that the lesson activities are congruent with the objectives.

Activities congruent with the objective

Figure 12: Major components of Simple Cooperation

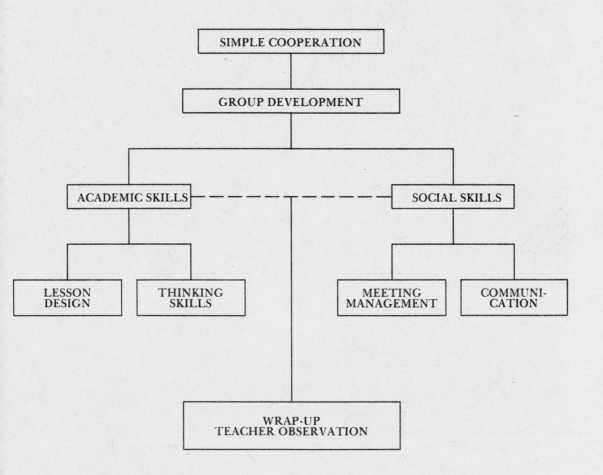

Figure 13: SOCIAL SKILLS COMPONENTS

```
                                          ┌─────────────────────────┐
                                          │  Social Norms & Values   │
                                          └─────────────────────────┘
                                          ┌─────────────────────────┐
                                          │   Classroom Standards    │
                                          └─────────────────────────┘
                        ┌──────────────┐
                        │ SOCIAL SKILLS│
                        └──────────────┘

┌──────────────────────────┐ - - - - - ┌──────────────────────┐
│   MEETING MANAGEMENT      │           │   COMMUNICATION       │
└──────────────────────────┘           └──────────────────────┘

┌──────┐ ┌──────┐ ┌───────────┐ ┌─────────┐ ┌─────────┐
│group │ │group │ │observation│ │ problem │ │decision │     ┌─────────┐ - - - ┌──────────┐
│ size │ │roles │ │           │ │ solving │ │ making  │     │ sending │       │receiving │
└──────┘ └──────┘ └───────────┘ └─────────┘ └─────────┘     └─────────┘       └──────────┘

                                                              ┌──────────────────┐
                                                              │     Verbal/       │
                                                              │    Nonverbal      │
                                                              │    Congruence     │
                                                              └──────────────────┘
```

NOTE: Social norms and values and classroom standards are integral aspects in the group development process. Therefore, they must be addressed as a prelude to the development of other social skills.

Figure 14

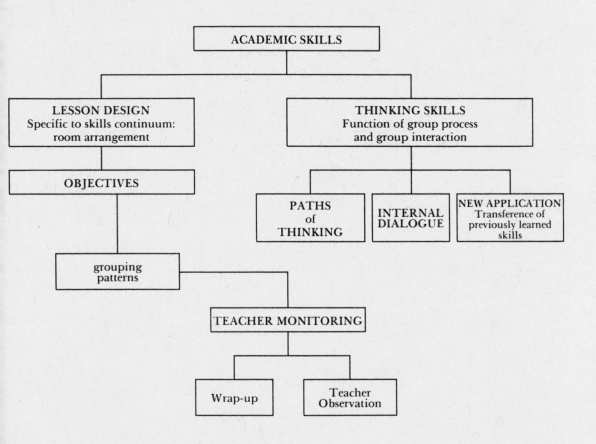

NOTE: Thinking skills may be taught in lesson design format. They may also be taught through the use of a thinking skills objective continuum.

Figure 15

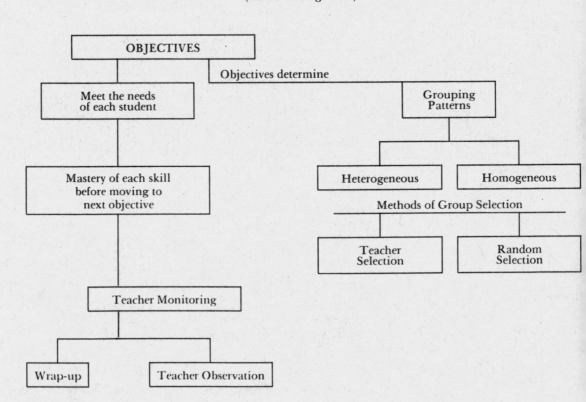

— Teach each social skill separately before integrating it into a Simple Cooperation lesson. A suggested continuum is provided (see Figure 16) to assist you in selecting the sequence of social skills instruction.

Teach social skills separately

— Remember that each objective will have it's own life cycle. For instance, an academic objective may be completed before mastery is obtained for the social skill objective. In that instance, the social skills objective would be incorporated into the next academic objective or vice versa. (This is graphically represented in Figure 17.)

Objective life cycle

Keeping these tenants in mind, it is now time to design your first lesson. A sample lesson plan format and instructions for completing the lesson plan are provided to assist you in this task. (See Figures 18.1 and 18.2.)

Completed sample lesson plans are provided for you to use as reference at the end of this chapter. You may want to redesign this format to meet your own individual needs. We encourage you to do so. Remember the "RIGHT" way to implement Simple Cooperation is the way that best meets the needs of you and your class.

Sample lessons

In Section II you will find a number of Social and Academic activities that we have used and found successful. We have written these activities in a general format so that you may easily translate the concepts into lesson plans that work for you and your students.

Social and academic activities

INTRODUCING SIMPLE COOPERATION TO STUDENTS

It is finally time for you to lead your first Simple Cooperation lesson. You have carefully laid the ground work by setting standards, getting acquainted, and adjusting those initial teacher standards with input from students. You have taught the social skill you are introducing into your academic lesson and have completed your lesson plan.

Groundwork

It is possible that you are a bit nervous right now, asking yourself, "How do I make this all come together smoothly?" Below, you will find a sequence of activities that will assist you in imple-

Figure 16: SOCIAL SKILLS CONTINUUM

1. SET STANDARDS
2. GET ACQUAINTED
3. GROUP MEMBER
4. SPEAKER GET ATTENTION OF RECEIVER
5. SPEAKER LOOK AT RECEIVER
6. LISTENER LOOK AT SENDER/SPEAKER
7. OWN THOUGHTS, IDEAS, FEELINGS
8. PRAISER
9. FACILITATOR AS MONITOR
10. LISTENER CLARIFY BY ASKING QUESTIONS
11. RECORDER FOR SINGLE ASSIGNMENT
12. TIME-KEEPER
13. CHECKER
14. '3-Cs' — SPEAKER BE CLEAR, CONCISE, COMPLETE
15. SPEAKER IDENTIFY FEELINGS BY NAME
16. LISTENER CLARIFY BY PARAPHRASING
17. FEEDBACK
18. OBSERVER
19. RECORDER FOR BRAINSTORMING, PROBLEM SOLVING
20. PERCEPTION CHECKING
21. NONVERBAL AWARENESS
22. CONGRUENCE: LISTENER
23. CONGRUENCE: SPEAKER
24. "I-MESSAGES"
25. DECISION MAKING
26. PROBLEM SOLVING
27. STUDENT FACILITATOR

Figure 17: INTEGRATION OF SOCIAL AND ACADEMIC OBJECTIVES

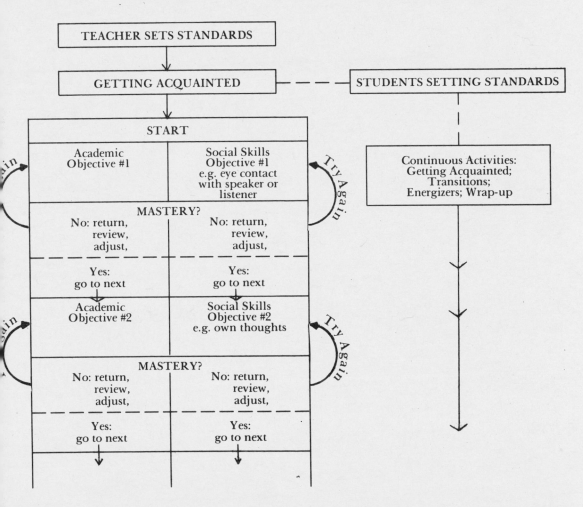

NOTE: Within the Simple Cooperation model, it would be possible to be on the 3rd academic objective while still working on the 1st social skill objective. OR, to be working on the 4th social skill objective while still on the 2nd academic objective. It is important not to rush students through the social skills continuum until they are ready to move on. Other activities, such as Getting Acquainted and Transition continue throughout the process. ALSO: Students setting standards may occur before beginning academic lessons OR may be interspersed at any and all appropriate times.

Figure 18.1: SIMPLE COOPERATION SAMPLE LESSON PLAN FORM

DATE(S):   TIME(S):   CLASS/SUBJECT:

ACADEMIC OBJECTIVE:

SOCIAL SKILL OBJECTIVE:

MATERIALS:

ROOM ARRANGEMENT:

GROUP SIZE: GROUPING PATTERNS:

GROUP ROLES:

GRADE/REWARD:

STUDENT OBSERVATION:

LESSON ACTIVITY:

WRAP UP:

TEACHER OBSERVATION:

Figure 18.2: INSTRUCTIONS FOR COMPLETING THE SIMPLE COOPERATION LESSON PLAN

1. DATE(S) and TIME(S): Write the date(s) and time(s) you are planning to present the lesson.

2. ACADEMIC OBJECTIVE: Write the ACADEMIC OBJECTIVE for the lesson.

3. SOCIAL SKILLS OBJECTIVE: Write the SOCIAL SKILLS objective for the lesson.

4. MATERIALS: List materials needed.

5. ROOM ARRANGEMENT: If there is a change in the present room arrangement, note the changes required.

6. GROUP SIZE: Write the number of students that are scheduled to be in each group.

7. GROUPING PATTERNS: Make a check mark after grouping patterns and write grouping information on the reverse side of the lesson plan (method of group selection, students assigned to each group, etc.)

8. GROUP ROLES: List the group roles to be used and the method chosen to assign the roles.

9. GRADE/REWARD: Note if completion of the assignment will result in a grade or reward and the criteria for receiving it. For example, "Each group that completes the assignment by the end of the period, will receive ten minutes free time on Friday". OR "The group product will receive a grade — each member of the group will receive that grade."

10. STUDENT OBSERVATION: List the specific behavior(s) to be observed. Attach the observation form to the lesson plan sheet.

11. LESSON ACTIVITY: Write the specific step by step procedure you will use to present the lesson including, when appropriate:
     — How you will introduce the lesson to the students — motivation, method of establishing meaning and relevance, etc.
     — How the new content will be presented — input of new material, method of modeling new skill, how you will check to make sure students understand the new skill, how they will practice the skill, and when and how the groups will work on the skill independently.

12. WRAP UP: List the specific WRAP UP activity to be used. If a WRAP UP sheet is to be used, attach to lesson plan.

13. TEACHER OBSERVATION: List the behavior you will be observing.

NOTE: All possible elements of a lesson plan are listed above. It is not necessary to include each element in every lesson. As in lessons you have prepared in the traditional manner, include only those elements appropriate for the specific content presented.

menting your first Simple Cooperation lesson. As with all Simple Cooperation activities, feel free to adjust this sequence to meet your needs. This is a sequence that has worked well for us in the past, it may not exactly fit you and your class, so adjust, create and have fun with your students during your first Simple Cooperation lesson.

— State the academic and social objectives to your class in terms that are appropriate to the age group. *State objective*

— Check for understanding. Make sure they know what they are supposed to do. *Check for understanding*

— Explain individual and/or group reward and/or grading system. *Reward/grading system*

— Let the students know which group they are to join and where that group will work. Again, this is done by preselected charting or a grouping activity. *Grouping directions*

— Before the lesson begins, tell the students what wrap-up activity will be used at the end of the lesson. This heightens their awareness that they will be accountable for a specific behavior or content area at the end of this lesson. *Wrap-up*

— If you have included teacher or student observation in the lesson, tell them about it, including what behaviors will be observed. *Observation*

— Instruct the students to join their groups. *Join groups*

— After all students have found their proper place in the room direct them to begin the activity. *Begin activity*

— While the students are working, move from group to group, facilitating discussion and problem solving. *Teacher facilitation*

— After the working time is over, conduct the planned wrap-up activity. *Wrap-up*

— When evaluating the lesson remember, if things didn't work out as well as you wanted, analyze what happened and try again. Simple Cooperation will work for you and your students — it just takes a little time to get going. *Evaluate*

SIMPLE COOPERATION
SAMPLE COMPLETED LESSON PLAN: #1

DATE(S): 10/15 - 10/19; TIME(S): 1:00-2:00 daily;
CLASS/SUBJECT: Grade 2 Social Studies

ACADEMIC OBJECTIVE: Each group will complete one section of the "Our School" mural.

SOCIAL OBJECTIVE: Each group member will "be on time."
In the classroom at 1:00 P.M. after lunch, and with his/her group
at designated teacher directed times during the lesson.

MATERIALS: Poster paint, butcher paper, construction paper,
crayons and scissors. (Appropriate materials will be placed at
each group's working space during lunch hour.)

ROOM ARRANGEMENT: No change.

GROUP SIZE: 3

GROUP ROLES: Group member
GROUPING PATTERNS: X

REWARD: Each group having each member seated in the
assigned working space after lunch and at teacher designated
times, will receive one sticker to be placed after the group name
on the bulletin board.

STUDENT OBSERVATON: None

LESSON ACTIVITY:

Day 1 — Lead a whole class discussion on why we have schools
and what is supposed to happen in schools. Take a walking tour
of the school, pointing out specific buildings and classrooms.

Day 2 — Introduce the mural concept, including what is to be on
the mural, etc. Divide the students into groups, assign each group
a specific building, playground equipment, etc., to draw. Students discuss and begin drawing the assignment.

Day 3 — Groups complete drawing, coloring, and cutting out
assignment. One group paints the background for the mural.

Day 4 — Conduct a whole class discussion on where the objects are to be placed on the mural. Make a notation on the mural showing where each group is to place their assignments as each building or object is discussed. Have groups place object on mural.

Day 5 — Invite visitors (principal, another class, the librarian, etc.) to the classroom to see the mural. If time allows, each group may discuss, one at a time, their section with the visitors. Conduct WRAP-UP.

WRAP-UP: One sentence WHIP. One new thing I learned about my school is...

TEACHER OBSERVATION: Whole class scan, using observation form listing all student names, after lunch and other times as appropriate.

REVERSE SIDE OF LESSON PLAN

HETEROGENEOUS GROUPING OF THREE: (Each group includes one identified high range, one middle range, and one low range achiever.)

Groups will be pre-assigned and placed on wall chart.

Group names will be consistent with the assigned task.

CAFETERIA GROUP: Suzanne, Cynthia, Clarence
AUDITORIUM GROUP: Michael, Mike, Cleo
WING 1 GROUP: Jenna, Margaret, Bill
WING 2 GROUP: David, Gregory, Pat
WING 3 GROUP: Billie Jo, Robert, Anthony
TREE GROUP: Tom, Virginia, Billy
FLOWER GROUP: Heath, Dawn, Tommy
MURAL GROUP: Robert, Jason, Kathy

SIMPLE COOPERATION
SAMPLE COMPLETED LESSON PLAN: #2

• Note: Groups formed for testing are identical to the study groups that have been working together for several weeks.

DATE(S): 10/21; TIME(S): 10:00-11:00;
CLASS/SUBJECT: Grade 9 History

ACADEMIC OBJECTIVE: Each group will complete one knowledge level test covering Chapters 9 & 10 of the text.

SOCIAL OBJECTIVE: Each group member will practice owning his/her own ideas, thoughts, and feelings (beginning sentence with "I")

MATERIALS: Text book, tests.

ROOM ARRANGEMENT: Movable desks in clusters of four.

GROUP SIZE: 4   **GROUPING PATTERNS:** X

GROUP ROLES: Group member, Praiser, Facilitator as Monitor, and Recorder for single assignment.

REWARD: Each group receiving 90% or better on the test will receive 20 minutes "extra" computer time. (5 minutes per person.) Group grade will be entered in the grade book.

STUDENT OBSERVATION: None

LESSON ACTIVITY:

— Ask student to be seated with their study groups.

— Opening: Assign each group the following task: Decide the most important reason you can think of for studying the information found in Chapters 9 & 10. (2 minutes individual thinking time, 5 minutes group discussion time, 3 minutes decision making time.) At the end of the time period the facilitator will share the decision with the class as a whole (5 minutes).

— Review testing process and decision making rules (5 minutes).

— Students take test (25 minutes)

— Wrap-Up

WRAP-UP: Wrap-up sheet (5 minutes).

TEACHER OBSERVATION: Observations of individual students — Owning own thoughts, opinions and feelings — Statements beginning with "I". (Observation process has been conducted during the study group session of previous days.)

WRAP-UP SHEET

Write a one sentence response to the following question and read it to the other members in the group.

One way I feel when I own my own thoughts, opinions and feelings is: _____

REVERSE SIDE OF LESSON PLAN

Heterogeneous groups of four. The groups were formed from the information obtained on a pretest given at the beginning of the week.

Study groups were formed, including one high, two middle and one low range achiever.

SUMMARY OF KEY POINTS

• Teacher observation and Wrap-up activities provide systematic methods for monitoring student progress in both academic and social skills areas.

• Group or individual student behaviors may be observed.

• Teacher observations help both the teacher and the students.

• A wrap-up activity follows each Simple Cooperation lesson.

• Wrap-up activities integrate thinking and communication skills.

• Wrap-up activities are directly related to the academic or social skill objective of the lesson.

• Wrap-up activities bring closure to the lesson.

• The room arrangement should be such that students can have direct eye contact with all others in their group.

• How to introduce students to Simple Cooperation was discussed.

• A sample lesson plan format was described.

• A suggested continuum of social skills previously discussed was provided to assist you with the sequence of instruction.

SECTION II

OVERVIEW

The following activities are offered as a resource and a place to begin. We encourage you to revise them to fit yourself and your students. We also encourage you to create others (and let us know about them).

The sample activities found in the social skills chapters are presented in basically the same sequence as the suggested social skills continuum.

We have provided a suggested grade level and materials needed for each activity. In many cases, and as appropriate, we have also identified the group roles necessary and an approximation of the amount of time needed to complete the activity. The time frame is based on our experience. The actual amount of time needed is dependent upon your particular group of students and your individualization of the content.

For example...there have been times when we scheduled an activity for 15 minutes and actually spent 45 minutes doing it. While this doesn't happen often, when it does it should never be considered 'a waste of time.' Sometimes students become much more involved in the activity's content than originally anticipated. Remember, social skills activities build trust and cohesion, and the more cohesive a group is the more it (and individual members) will achieve and accomplish.

Another point to remember in terms of time is that we, as teachers, NEVER have enough time. Whether we're teaching at the preschool or college level, we are typically wishing that we had "just a little more time." But...

For the most part, we have not provided time frames for the academic activities. The actual amount of time needed will vary according to the content of the lesson, the skill level of the students, and the amount of time you and your class have been practicing Simple Cooperation.

ONE FINAL POINT TO REMEMBER:

Before beginning an activity always check to insure that your students understand your instructions. Assuring that students understand where they should go, what group they belong to, what they are to do and why they are doing it will greatly enhance the learning that occurs. It is also a critical element in the activity's success. You may want to review Chapter 6 for methods of checking for understanding.

CHAPTER 7

GETTING ACQUAINTED, TRANSITION, AND ENERGIZERS

Many activities are interchangeable as Getting Acquainted, Transition, or Energizers. Bracketed notes[ ] reflect the primary use of each activity.

INTRODUCTIONS [Getting Acquainted]

ROLE(S): None

TIME: 20-35 minutes

GRADE LEVEL: K-Adult

MATERIALS: Charted directions

A chart is constructed listing specific information that the teacher would like the students in the class to know about each other; such as name, hobby, favorite TV program, etc. The number and complexity of the items on the chart is dependent upon the grade level, attention span of the students and the time available to complete the activity.

Students choose a partner with whom they are least acquainted. Each student interviews his/her partner for five minutes, obtaining the specified information. At the end of the ten minute interview period, the students take turns introducing their partners to the entire class.

— — —

THE MEMORY GAME [Getting Acquainted]

GRADE LEVEL: Grade 2-Adult

ROLE(S): None

TIME: 20-30 minutes

MATERIALS: None

The class, including the teacher, is seated in a circle. Students beginning at the immediate right of the teacher recite the alphabet in sequence, each student saying only one letter of the alphabet. The sound of the letter that each student says becomes her/his beginning sound with which to choose an adjective that best describes him/herself.

The students are given one or two minutes to choose an adjective such as Affable Jane, Bouncy Mary, etc.

After the adjectives have been chosen, the students take turns, again beginning at the teacher's right, introducing themselves by adjective and first name.

VARIATION #1: After going full circle, the process is repeated with the added task of stating the names of all the students that have taken their turns before.

Jane, the first student on the teacher's right, will say only her adjective and name, Affable Jane. Mary will say Affable Jane, Bouncy Mary, while the third student must say Affable Jane and Bouncy Mary before stating her/his own name.

VARIATION #2: It is also possible to include in the directions that the student to the immediate right and left can whisper answers in their classmates ear if they get stuck.

VARIATION #3: The adjectives may begin with the first letter of the student's name rather than a letter of the alphabet.

NOTE: The teacher may wish to seat students he/she knows have short term memory disorders to her/his right to avoid putting these students "on the spot" by requiring them to remember more names than they may be capable of.

— — —

GETTING ACQUAINTED CARDS [Getting Acquainted, Transition]

GRADE LEVEL: Grade 2-Adult

ROLE(S): None

TIME: 20-25 minutes

MATERIALS: Name tags or 3x5 index cards (pins or tape is needed if index cards are used), charted directions, charted sample Getting Acquainted Card(s).

Each student is given an identity card (name tag or index card) and is instructed to write her/his first name in the center of the card. Students then complete their cards by following the instructions on the charted sample identity card (See Figure 19).

You may want to assist the students in this process by verbally walking them through the activity.

— In the upper right hand corner of the card write the name of the last place you vacationed.

— In the lower right hand corner write the number of brothers and sisters you have.

— In the lower left hand corner write the name of your favorite TV program.

— In the upper left hand corner write the city where you were born.

The completed Getting Acquainted Card is attached to the writer's shirt or blouse. Students are then broken into groups of three or four. Group members share the information on their Getting Acquainted Card.

VARIATION: This can be done in pairs, larger groups, or with the entire class.

— — —

GUESS WHO [Getting Acquainted, Transition]

GRADE LEVEL: Preschool-Adult

ROLE(S): None

TIME: 15 minutes, plus time at the end of the day

MATERIALS: 5x7 drawing paper, marking pens, pencils or crayons.

After paper and drawing instruments are distributed students are instructed to draw a picture of him/herself, which includes definite clues to her/his idenity. Since these are secret portraits, some type of privacy is needed, such as a learning center (or use as a homework assignment).

Figure 19: SAMPLE IDENTITY CARD

city where born	last vacation place
NAME	
favorite TV program	# brothers/sisters

— —

SAMPLE COMPLETED IDENTITY CARD

Brooklyn	Ashland, Oregon
PEGGY	
Good Morning America	2 brothers

After portraits are completed they are hung on the wall with a blank sheet of paper immediately below. During the day, students review the portraits and write who they think each one is on the paper provided. It may be helpful if a list of class members is posted to use as a reference for correct spelling or names they do not remember.

At the end of the day each student signs her/his portrait.

— — —

ONE NEW FACT [Getting Acquainted, Transition]

GRADE LEVEL: Preschool-Adult

ROLE(S): None

TIME: 20-25 minutes

MATERIALS: None

Students are seated randomly in a circle and instructed to tell one fact they have learned this year about the person on his/her right. The only restriction is that it must be a positive statement about the person.

The teacher leads the activity by stating one new fact about the person on his/her right, and the process is continued around the circle until the student to the teacher's left tells one new fact about the teacher.

— — —

THE WHIP [Transition, Energizer]

GRADE LEVEL: Preschool-Adult

ROLE(S): None

TIME: 10-15 minutes

MATERIALS: None

Students are requested to formulate a one word response to an open ended question constructed by the teacher; e.g. "A one word description of how I am feeling this moment is..." Students are given a minute or two to think of their response.

The option of passing is always given to the students. (There are times when students may feel threatened by the question or may not be able to formulate the response within the required time parameters.) In the event that the student wishes to pass she/he simply says, "I pass" and the teacher moves on to the next student.

Neither the teacher nor the class members are to react or respond. All answers are accepted with a simple "thank you" by the teacher, without further comment or request for clarification.

VARIATION: Instead of a one word response a short phrase, one sentence, or several sentences may be requested.

IT IS IMPORTANT TO CLARIFY EXACTLY WHAT TYPE OF RESPONSE IS REQUIRED BEFORE BEGINNING THE ACTIVITY.

Sample WHIP questions are:

1) My favorite sport is...
2) One new fact I learned during class yesterday is...
3) My favorite vacation spot is...
4) My favorite subject in school is...

— — —

AARDVARKS AND ANTELOPES [Transition, Energizer]

GRADE LEVEL: Grade 5-Adult

ROLE(S): None

TIME: 20-40 minutes

MATERIALS: One object that symbolizes the Aardvark and one that symbolizes the Antelope

The class, including the teacher, is seated in a circle.

The teacher has in her/his possession two objects. One object he/she will call an aardvark the other an antelope.

— The teacher turns to her/his right and says to Student #1 "This is an aardvark"

— Student #1 asks the teacher, "A what?"

— The Teacher replies, "An aardvark" and hands the object to the student.

— Student #1 then turns to Student #2 on his/her right and says, "This is an aardvark."

— Student #2 asks, "A what?"

— Student #1 turns to the teacher and asks, "A what?"

— The teacher replies, "An aardvark"

— Student #1 turns to Student #2 and says, "This is an aardvark" and hands the object to Student #2.

In other words each time the aardvark is given to the next student in the circle, the question "A what" must be passed back around the circle to the teacher. The teacher answers, "An aardvark". The answer "An aardvark" is passed back around the circle until it reaches the person in possession of the aardvark. When the student has received the answer, she/he may then turn to the next student and state, "This is an aardvark."

The process is repeated until the "aardvark" is passed from one student to another, full circle, back around to the teacher.

As soon as the teacher is sure that the aardvark is moving smoothly counter-clockwise around the circle, and the students are following the correct procedure, he/she hands the object that is to be the antelope to the student on the left and says, "This is an antelope."

The antelope then begins its' trek in a clockwise direction around the circle in the same manner.

In other words, while the aardvark is making its trek counter-clockwise around the circle, the antelope is moving simultaneously around the circle in a clockwise fashion.

The activity is completed when both the aardvark and the antelope have gone full circle and are in the teacher's possession.

— — —

FOCUS WORKSHEET [Getting Acquainted, Transition, Energizer]

GRADE LEVEL: Grade 2-Adult

ROLE(S): None

TIME: 10-20 minutes

MATERIALS: A pre-prepared worksheet on which 5-10 questions have been listed. The questions may be academic, social, trivia or a combination thereof. (See Figure 20)

The worksheets are distributed to the students. They are instructed to complete the worksheet by interviewing fellow students. They may not obtain more than one answer from each student they interview. A specific amount of time is given to complete the activity, such as 5 to 15 minutes depending on the complexity and number of questions.

Be prepared for a lot of movement and a relatively high noise level for this activity.

At the end of the activity you may wish to have the students "turn in" the worksheet, or share the information they have obtained with a partner or small group.

— — —

EXERCISES [Transition, Energizers]

GRADE LEVEL: Preschool-Adult

ROLE(S): None

TIME: 5-10 minutes

MATERIALS: None

In this activity the teacher leads the class in specific physical exercises such as stretching, bending over, etc., as appropriate for the grade level taught. (Note: This is one of Peggy's favorite activities when conducting adult workshops — everyone has fun!)

VARIATION: The teacher leads the class in Simon Says. This works especially well if you are teaching in tight quarters. Examples include "Simon says touch your nose." "Simon says touch your left shoulder with your right thumb."

— — —

Figure 20: SAMPLE FOCUS WORKSHEET

INSTRUCTIONS:

a. Find someone who can answer the following questions or fits the description.

b. Have that person sign in the appropriate place.

c. Each question/description should be signed by a different person.

— —

1. What is paraphrasing? _____

2. Describe the major stages of group development. _____

3. Someone wearing blue. _____

4. What does a 'praiser' do? _____

5. What is the first step in problem solving? _____

6. Someone wearing shoes that tie. _____

GUESS THAT NUMBER [Transition, Energizer]

GRADE LEVEL: Grade 2-Adult

ROLE(S): None

TIME: 15-20 minutes

MATERIALS: Name tags on which random numbers are written; three questions charted or written on the blackboard.

Numbers between 1 and 1,000 are written on name tags (number range may be adjusted to the ability level of the students) and then one is placed on each student's back. It is important that the student does not see his/her own number.

Each person is instructed to discover his/her own number.

She/he may do so by asking any of the following three questions:

1) Is my number lower than...?
2) Is my number higher than...?
3) Is my number...?

Student than "mill" around the room asking only one question of each person. When a student has "discovered" his/her number he/she may be seated.

At the end of the time period, all students are seated. Students who have not yet discovered their numbers may elect to continue the discovery process during recess or break time, or they may be told their number.

— — —

BEES [Energizer]

GRADE LEVEL: Kindergarten-Adult

ROLE(S): None

TIME: 1-2 minutes

MATERIALS: None

All group members mimic the sound of bees (zzzzzzz) beginning very softly and increasing in loudness.

— — —

APPLAUSE: [Energizer]

GRADE LEVEL: Kindergarten-Adult

ROLE(S): None

TIME: 1 minute

MATERIALS: None

Group members simply applaud for about 15 seconds.

SOURCES

INTRODUCTIONS: Original source unknown.

THE MEMORY GAME: Original source unknown.

GETTING ACQUAINTED: Original source unknown.

GUESS WHO: Jacquie

ONE NEW FACT: Adapted by Peggy and Jacquie from various activities they have experienced and conducted in times past. Original source unknown.

THE WHIP: Developed by Dr. Stan Schainker, Associate Superintendent, San Francisco Unified School District, San Francisco, CA.

AARDVARKS AND ANTELOPES: Original source unknown.

FOCUS WORKSHEET: Original source unknown.

EXERCISES: Adapted for use as an energizer by Peggy.

GUESS THAT NUMBER: Jacquie.

BEES: Original source unknown.

CHAPTER 8
ACADEMIC ACTIVITIES

COMMENTS:

These are general activity formats that can easily be translated into any subject matter. You may find it necessary to make adaptations for your particular group of students. However, we have found the general format works well for most groups. The amount of time necessary for each activity varies depending on the content, student skill level and how long you and your students have been involved in Simple Cooperation.

MATCHING

GRADE LEVEL: Preschool-Grade 2

ROLE(S): None

MATERIALS: Two-piece jigsaw puzzles.

Students are grouped in pairs or triads and assigned to a workspace. The pieces necessary for one puzzle per student are mixed up and placed face down in front of each group. Students are given a specific amount of time (such as 5 or 10 minutes) to turn the pieces face up and assemble the puzzles correctly.

— — —

MURALS

GRADE LEVEL: Preschool-Grade 9

ROLE(S): None

MATERIALS: Varied, depending on the type of mural the class is making. Commonly used materials are butcher paper, poster paint, marking pens, paste, scissors, sample pictures or stencils of objects to be put on mural.

This activity is appropriate after a series of lessons on any subject that lends itself to visual representation; such as, farms, gardens, maps, etc.

Students are divided into groups of two or three. Each group is given the assignment to complete one section of the mural. For instance, if the assignment is to make a mural of a farm, one group would draw the background, including the sky, grass and dirt; another group would make the chickens out of construction paper; another the cows; and so on. Instructions as to the relative size of the objects should be given if stencils are not used.

After each group has completed the assignment, the teacher assist the class in attaching all of the completed mural parts to the background.

— — —

BUILDING THE ALPHABET

GRADE LEVEL: Preschool-Grade 2

ROLE(S): Checker

MATERIALS: Alphabet tiles or write the alphabet on construction paper squares.

Students are divided into groups of two or three and given the alphabet tiles which have been mixed up. Within a specified amount of time, each group is to arrange the tiles in correct sequential order beginning with A and ending with Z.

At the end of the allocated time, an answer sheet is given to the checker, and the group reviews its answers for accuracy.

VARIATION: Any task which requires sequencing may be presented in this activity format.

— — —

DRAWING A SPECIAL PICTURE

GRADE LEVEL: Preschool-Age 6

ROLE(S): None

MATERIALS: Construction or drawing paper, crayons or marking pens.

The students are grouped into pairs and instructed to decide on a topic for the special picture they will draw. The teacher then checks to make sure that each pair has chosen the subject area.

The pairs then work together for a given length of time to complete their special picture.

— — —

STUDY GROUPS

GRADE LEVEL: Grade 2-Adult

ROLE(S): Checker

MATERIALS: 20 index cards, numbered 1-20; a list of 20 questions and answers, stated briefly.

Students are divided into groups of three or four. Groups may be heterogeneous or homogeneous, depending on the objective of the lesson.

Three roles are assigned to the group: 1) the checker, 2) the test-taker, and 3) the challenger. If there are more than three members in the group all the remaining members become challengers. These roles are rotated in a clockwise manner during this activity. (NOTE: The roles of "test-taker" and "challenger" are not routine group roles. Their purpose is self-evident in the following text.)

A specific amount of time is allocated for the study session (10-20 minutes is a time frame that works well).

During the study session the following procedure is followed:

— The stack of index cards are shuffled and placed face down on the center of the table.

— The test-taker draws a card and places it face up on the table.

— The checker reads the number and locates the corresponding number on the question/answer sheet.

— The checker reads the question to the test-taker.

— The test-taker answer the question.

— The checker asks if there are any challenges. This is done whether the answer is correct or incorrect. Challengers then tell the checker their version of the correct answer.

— The checker then tells the group who has stated the correct answer. The person with the correct answer may keep the numbered card that has been drawn.

— If there are no correct answers, the test-taker places the card he/she has drawn at the bottom of the stack on the table, and the checker reads the correct answer.

— There is a penalty for an incorrect challenge. If a person has challenged and his/her answer is incorrect he/she must place one of the cards he/she has previously won at the bottom of the stack. Therefore, in order to challenge an answer, the challenger must have already "won" a card.

— Round #1 of the study session is then complete. The roles are rotated in a clockwise manner, the checker hands the answer sheet to the person on his/her left and the process is repeated.

When beginning this activity it is helpful to write the group role assignment on index cards. The cards can then be rotated in a clockwise fashion after each round to assist students in remembering their roles.

NOTE: Study questions and answers must be clear, concise and to the point. To avoid confusion, students should be required to answer in the extact words listed on the answer sheet. Spelling, math facts and other knowledge level questions, such as "Who invented the cotton gin?", lend themselves to this activity.

— — —

WRITING ASSIGNMENTS

GRADE LEVEL: Grades 2-Adults

ROLE(S): Recorder (Optional: facilitator and/or time-keeper.)

TIME: 30-45 minutes

MATERIALS: Pencils and paper.

This activity may follow a direct lesson on any subject.

Students are divided into heterogeneous or homogeneous groups of 2-3.

The first task of the group is to discuss the subject assigned and to decide on content. A facilitator and recorder may be assigned to assist the group in decision making. Brainstorming may be appropriate. The discussion period may last from 5-15 minutes depending upon the complexity of the task. A time-keeper may be assigned to each group or the teacher may act as time-keeper for the class.

The second task is to begin writing. A recorder is assigned to write down the group product. The group may work together and develop a product by consensus decision making or take turns writing each sentence or line of poetry. 15-30 minutes are provided for writing.

The final task of the group is to review the assignment and make any corrections or changes necessary. Each member then signs his/her name on the finished product to indicate agreement.

When completed, the recorder reads the assignment to the class.

— — —

GROUP TESTING

GRADE LEVEL: Grade 2-Adult

ROLE(S): Facilitator and Recorder

MATERIALS: Group test, text book and other appropriate information; pencils and paper.

Heterogeneous or homogeneous group of 2-5 students are formed, depending upon the objectives and structure in which the students have been working.

A single group grade is appropriate for this activity.

The group test is usually an open book test with one group grade. It is appropriate to follow up the group test with a similar individual test and utilize the group test as a learning activity.

Copies of the test are given to each student. Each test question is discussed by the group, If there is doubt regarding the correct answer, the students may refer to available reference material.

The facilitator assists the group in arriving at a consensus decision on each answer and the recorder writes the answer on the final answer sheet that is to be given to the teacher. It is a good idea for the recorder to read the answer to the group to make sure that she/he has recorded it correctly.

All group members sign the test to indicate agreement with the responses before giving it to the teacher for grading.

Be sure to keep the test relatively short and allow ample time to complete the assignment. Group testing usually takes longer; however, when students have completed the assignment you can be sure that they will know a lot more than when they began. And after all, isn't that what we are all about?

— — —

GROUP RESEARCH PROJECTS AND REPORTS

GRADE LEVEL: Grade 3-Adult

ROLE(S): Facilitator and Recorder

MATERIALS: Group assignment sheet, research materials, paper and pencils.

Students are formed into heterogeneous groups of 3-5, depending upon the objectives and grade level of the students. Each student is given an assignment specific to his/her ability level.

A single group grade is appropriate for this activity.

This is an ideal method of utilizing the strengths of each group member in the areas of task completion, modalities and thinking skills. Each member is given a specific assignment for which materials are available on her/his ability level.

For instance, if the research project focused on the westward movement, one member of the group may be assigned to research famous scouts and be required to make a list of names and famous deeds. The second member may analyze the economic impact of the westward movement on the economy, while the third would research the impact of the westward movement on the Native American population.

A facilitator and recorder are assigned to each group.

A research assignment may last as long as a week, sometimes even more time is required. A sample schedule for the project is:

— Day 1 — The facilitator reviews the assignment with the group to ensure that each member is fully aware of the components of the assignment, including content and location of reference material.

— Days 2 & 3 — Team members work independently on their respective assignments, gathering information and taking notes.

— Day 4 — The members regroup and discuss what they have learned, each member giving a "report" to the other members.

— Day 5 — The group report is written, using the instructions on the assignment sheet as a guideline. The facilitator leads the discussion and the recorder writes the group answer. After completion of the assignment, the recorder reads the report aloud to the group. All group members must sign the report to indicate agreement with the responses before the report is turned in to the teacher.

— — —

FORMING AN OPINION

GRADE LEVEL: Grade 4-Adult

ROLE(S): Facilitator, Recorder, Time-Keeper

TIME: 1-2 hours

MATERIALS: Information sheets, class lecture, or film on a controversial issue relevant to the curriculum or a current event.

Heterogeneous groups of 3-5 students are formed. A facilitator, recorder and time-keeper are chosen for each group.

Students are instructed to discuss the pros and cons of the issue presented. The recorder writes down major points of the discussion on a large chart which is divided into two sections, pros and cons.

10-20 minutes are provided for group discussion. The facilitator makes sure that each group member has a turn to state his/her opinions and thoughts. The recorder writes the key points under either the pro or con section of the chart.

Another 10-20 minutes are provided for students to discuss the charted information and come to a consensus decision on what "stand" they wish to take on the issue. (You might want to review the problem solving/decision making processes described in Section I.)

The goal is to have each group reach a consensus decision within the allotted time frame.

At the end of the time period, the facilitator of each group reports the group's decision and the rationale behind the decision to the rest of the class. If the group has been unable to arrive at a consensus decision, the facilitator shares that fact with the class and discusses the problems they encountered in their decision making process.

— — —

THE GREAT DEBATE

GRADE LEVEL: Grade 4-Adult

ROLE(S): Facilitator and Recorder (Optional: Time-Keeper)

TIME: 35-50 minutes

MATERIALS: Information sheets, class lecture, or film on a given controversial issue.

The class is divided in half, forming two debate teams. Each team is assigned a position on the issue at hand. For example, the issue may be abortion. One team is assigned to take the pro-abortion stand, regardless of the individual member's personal opinions on the issue; the other team will take the stand against abortion.

A facilitator and a recorder are assigned from each team.

A 20-30 minute time period is allotted for the teams to discuss the critical factors involved in their assigned position. The recorder writes down relevant information on the blackboard or chart paper.

Two chairs are placed at the front of the room. The remaining chairs are pulled to either side, leaving an aisle in the center. Team members sit with their respective teams. The teams are facing each other.

THE GREAT DEBATE BEGINS!

A 15-20 minute period is set for the debate. The ground rules for the debate are:

— In order to speak, a team member must sit in the debate chair.

— The teams alternate speakers. Speakers may talk no longer than 1 minute. The teacher may choose to take on the role of time-keeper or pre-select a student before dividing up the teams.

— Each team member must speak before the time period is up.

— A speaker may speak more than once.

— There must always be a team member in the debate chair.

— In order to take a place in the debate chair, the team member must walk up to the person sitting in the chair and tap her/him on the shoulder. The member in the chair is allowed to finish his/her sentence or thought, and then must move out of the chair and allow the other team member to be seated.

— If more than one team member wants to take his/her place in the debate chair, the facilitator helps by establishing a waiting line, insuring that everyone has a turn to speak.

— It is the facilitator's job to make sure that each team member sits in the debate chair at least one time.

When the debate time has ended a wrap-up session is conducted.

— — —

GROUP WORKSHEET

GRADE LEVEL: Grade 1-Adult

ROLE(S): Facilitator, Recorder, Time-Keeper

MATERIALS: Assigned worksheet.

Students are divided into heterogeneous or homogeneous groups of 3-5, depending on the objective of the lesson.

A facilitator, recorder and time-keeper are chosen for each group.

Individual worksheets are distributed to ALL group members. A group answer sheet is given to each group. It is important that each group member has the same worksheet as the other group members. The worksheet may, however, vary from group to group. It is possible for each group to have a different worksheet.

A specific amount of time is allocated for each group member to work on his/her worksheet alone. The students then share their answers with the other members of the group. The facilitator insures that each student in the group has input during the discussion time.

Each question on the worksheet is addressed one at a time. A consensus decision on the correct answer is made. The recorder writes the chosen response on the group answer sheet, reading it back to the group to make sure that he/she has recorded the answer correctly.

After completion of the assignment, all group members sign the answer sheet to indicate agreement with the responses before turning it in to the teacher.

SOURCES:

Matching: Jacquie

Murals: Jacquie

Building the Alphabet: Jacquie

Draw A Special Picture: Original source unknown

Study Groups: Adapted by Peggy and Jacquie for Simple Cooperation from their personal study group experiences. Peggy first experienced this concept as a Doctorial Candidate at the University of La Verne; Jacquie, in an 11th grade history class. Original source unknown.

Writing Assignments: Adapted for Simple Cooperation by Jacquie and Peggy, who have experienced group writing assignments as students and have, in turn, used this concept in workshops. Original source unknown.

Group Testing: Adapted for Simple Cooperation by Peggy and Jacquie. Original source unknown.

Group Research and Project Reports: Adapted for Simple Cooperation by Jacquie and Peggy. Peggy's first exposure to this concept was at The University of La Verne; Jacquie's in 11th grade history. Original source unknown.

Forming An Opinion: Peggy and Jacquie.

The Great Debate: Adapted for Simple Cooperation by Jacquie and Peggy from the many debates they participated in while attending school. The original source of "Debate" unknown.

Group Worksheet: Adapted for Simple Cooperation by Peggy and Jacquie. Original source unknown.

CHAPTER 9
WRAP-UP ACTIVITIES

FEEDBACK CARDS

GRADE LEVEL: Grade 1-Adult

ROLE(S): None

TIME: 3-5 minutes

MATERIALS: 3x5 index cards

At the close of the activity group members write down their response to the lesson.

Feedback cards are used most often for open-ended reactions. However, the teacher may ask students to respond to a specific question or direction such as "Write down the number of times you praised another group member during this work period." or "Write down one new rule that you have learned today about punctuating sentences."

In most instances feedback cards are anonymous; however, there may be times when it would be helpful to have students sign their cards. The teacher must use his/her judgment when making this decision — anonymous cards tend to elicit a higher degree of directness and honesty.

— — —

SMALL GROUP DISCUSSION

GRADE LEVEL: Kindergarten-Adult

ROLE(S): Optional: Facilitator

TIME: 5-10 minutes

MATERIALS: None

Groups of 2-5 students are directed to discuss a specific topic such as; "One way our group worked together to accomplish its objective today is..." or "The most interesting part of the science assignment was...," for 2-3 minutes.

Allow a minute or so of private "thinking time" before beginning the group discussion. If time permits, the facilitator of each group may share his/her group's answers with the class as a whole.

— — —

THE COMPLIMENT

GRADE LEVEL: Kindergarten-Adult

ROLE(S): None

TIME: 5-10 minutes

MATERIALS: None

Within their Simple Cooperation group, each group member is directed to give one compliment to the person on his/her right about how she/he has helped the group accomplish the task.

Compliments should begin with one group member — for instance, the group member sitting closest to the wall clock, and continue around the circle. This ensures that each group member hears all the compliments and that two people are not talking at once.

— — —

THE WRAP-UP SHEET

GRADE LEVEL: Grade 2-Adult

ROLE(S): None

TIME: 10 minutes

MATERIALS: Prepared wrap-up sheet

A pre-written wrap-up sheet is distributed to the class with 1-5 specific questions which each student must answer. The questions should lend themselves to short responses. Figure 21 displays three possible wrap-up sheets.

Individually, students take 2-5 minutes writing their own responses to the questions.

At the end of the response time, students may be asked to give

Figure 21: SAMPLE WRAP-UP SHEETS

Sample #1

WRAP-UP

To me, the most important parts of this lesson were:

_____

_____

_____
— —

Sample #2

WRAP-UP

Circle the number that best describes your feeling about how much YOU contributed to the group product today.

LOW								HIGH	
1	2	3	4	5	6	7	8	9	10

— —

Sample #3

WRAP-UP

Complete the drawing that shows how you feel about today's group lesson.

— —

their response sheets to the teacher or to read their answers out loud to the class or small group.

— — —

THE FANTASY

GRADE LEVEL: Grade 2-Adult

ROLE(S): None

TIME: 15 minutes

MATERIALS: None

Students are asked to let their imaginations stretch and to create new ideas relevant to the topic they have just been working with.

For example, if they have been studying a unit on famous inventors, they would be asked to fantasize that they were famous inventors themselves and imagine a fantastic invention that they would like to create.

Students are given a minute or two "thinking time" and then write the name of their invention on paper.

Students then share their new invention with their group or with the whole class, as time permits.

SOURCES:

Feedback Cards: Original source unknown

Small Group Discussion: Adapted for Simple Cooperation, by Peggy and Jacquie from many experiences each have had as students and workshop leaders.

The Compliment: Original source unknown.

Wrap-up Sheet: Adapted for Simple Cooperation by Jacquie who first experienced a variation of this concept while enrolled in a sociology class. Original source unknown.

The Fantasy: Jacquie.

CHAPTER 10
COMMUNICATION ACTIVITIES

LISTENING: NONVERBAL CONGRUENCE

Part 1 — EXPERIENCING INATTENTIVENESS

GRADE LEVEL: Kindergarten-Adult

TIME: 20-30 minutes

MATERIALS: None

Heterogeneous or homogeneous groups of 3 are formed and remain together for Parts 1 and 2 of this activity.

One group member begins talking about something — perhaps their favorite activity. The "listeners" are directed to pay no attention to the speaker. Instead, they are to look around the room, doodle, and/or begin reading.

Allow 2 minutes for each person to talk; then rotate roles. Continue until each group member has been the speaker.

The groups discuss how it felt to be speaking with no one paying attention.

Part 2: EXPERIENCING ATTENTIVENESS

One group member begins talking about something — perhaps his/her last vacation. The listeners pay close attention to the speaker, exhibiting eye contact, leaning forward to listen better, nodding their heads, as appropriate.

The group then discusses how it felt to be listened to.

Part 3: CLASS DISCUSSION

A full class discussion is then held, focusing on the different feelings between the two situations.

— — —

LISTENING: THE ROTTEN CHICKEN

GRADE LEVEL: Kindergarten-Adult

ROLE(S): None

TIME: 1 hour

MATERIALS: THE ROTTEN CHICKEN, drawing paper, crayons.

THE ROTTEN CHICKEN is read aloud to the class. A specific discussion question is presented to the class by the teacher. The class discusses the question together.

Students are then broken into dyads and instructed to do the following:

1) Decide how to depict the group's feeling response to the question.

2) With all group members participating, draw a picture representing the feeling response to the question.

3) If there is disagreement in the group as to how the feeling is to be depicted, this should be reflected in the drawing.

Sample questions to ask the class include:

— How do you act when you feel rotten?

— How does it feel when you believe in yourself?

— How did the willow tree feel after it helped the hen?

— How did the young rooster's feelings change about himself and his mother?

After the pictures are completed they may be posted on a bulletin board as an end it itself, or used as a kick-off for further discussion.

THE ROTTEN CHICKEN is a story that can be interpreted on many levels. While written in a format appropriate for children, inherent in the story line are themes of adult complexity, among which is psychological abuse. This title is offered as an example of the use of literature in listening skills activities. The teacher should select titles that are a "best fit" for her/his class.

Suggested criteria for story selection are:

— Brief in length, taking no longer than 5-10 minutes to read.

— Contains a message that elicits a feeling response.

— Contains pre-made discussion questions, in order to shorten preparation time.

— — —

LISTENING: CLARIFYING BY ASKING QUESTIONS

LEARNING TO ASK QUESTIONS

GRADE LEVEL: Kindergarten-Adult

ROLE(S): None

TIME: 30 minutes

MATERIALS: Short story or newspaper item.

The teacher reads a short story or news item to the class, leaving out at least half the critical facts of the story. Students then ask questions to gain the necessary facts. The teacher responds to each specific question without volunteering additional information. Following this activity, the class reviews the questions that were asked and discusses which questions resulted in gaining the most information; then examines how those questions were phrased.

— — —

PARAPHRASING

The following three activities will help students learn how to clarify by paraphrasing.

ACTIVITY 1:

GRADE LEVEL: Grade 2-Adult

ROLE(S): None

TIME: 10-15 minutes

MATERIALS: None

In pairs, one student tells the other what he/she did over the weekend and how he/she felt about it. The second student, the listener, paraphrases the message. The speaker responds by validating the listener's interpretation of the message or clarifies his/her message.

Switch roles and repeat.

ACTIVITY 2:

GRADE LEVEL: Grade 4-Adult

ROLE(S): None

TIME: 10-15 minutes

MATERIALS: Any printed matter

Using any printed material (i.e. book, newspaper, magazine) students in groups of 3 or 4 read a short paragraph (2-4 sentences) and paraphrase the content.

ACTIVITY 3:

GRADE LEVEL: Grade 4-Adult

ROLE(S): None

TIME: 15-20 minutes

MATERIALS: Student generated short stories.

Using short stories students have previously written, pair off with one student paraphrasing the other's short story.

The original author verifies the correctness of the reader's interpretation. OR, if the interpretation is incorrect, clarifies.

Switch roles after 5-10 minutes.

(This also helps students learn how to write more clearly.)

— — —

SPEAKING — CONGRUENCE, VERBAL/NONVERBAL: ON BECOMING AN ACTOR

GRADE LEVEL: Grade 2-Adult

ROLE(S): None

TIME: 30 minutes

MATERIALS: Charted poem or tongue-twister (should be at an easy reading level for all students), 15 - 3x5 index cards with one affect or behavior written on each card (e.g. happy, sad, disgusted, surprised, etc.)

The charted brief poem or tongue-twister (e.g. Sister Suzie sews sample skirts.) is placed within easy view of all students. The teacher practices reading the chart with the students to ensure its' readability.

The deck of affect cards is placed in a stack on the table. Students take turns going to the front of the class and drawing a card — no one else should see the card.

The student reads the chart, using the intonation appropriate for the affect stated on the card.

The class then attempts to guess the affect conveyed.

VARIATION: Students may be divided into smaller groups.

— — —

SPEAKING — CONGRUENCE VERBAL/NONVERBAL:
ON BECOMING A POET

GRADE LEVEL: Grade 2-Adult

ROLE(S): None

TIME: 15-25 minutes

MATERIALS: ½ sheet of paper for each student, pencils.

Students are grouped in pairs. Each group decides who is to be #1 and who is to be #2.

Without looking at each other's paper, the #1's are asked to write down their greatest wish or fantasy. The #2's are asked to write down the most perfect place, activity or circumstance they can think of.

The pairs then read their newly made poem aloud to the class, hearing it for the first time themselves: #1 reading his/her section first, followed quickly by #2.

Sample poem: (#1) — "I would like to be floating on clouds in the sky...(#2) eating chocolate ice cream."

— — —

COMBINED LISTENING AND SPEAKING:

THE VERBAL MAP

GRADE LEVEL: Kindergarten-Adult

ROLE(S): None

TIME: 10-20 minutes

MATERIALS: None

Students pair up. One student, the speaker, gives verbal directions from the classroom to the office/restroom/playground, or some other campus location. The second student, the listener, follows these directions exactly as given, and reports if he/she actually arrived at the desired location.

Follow this activity with a discussion about what went right or wrong pointing out the necessity for clarity when speaking, and clarifying when listening.

— — —

COMBINED LISTENING AND SPEAKING:

NEWS REPORTER

GRADE LEVEL: Grade 3-Adult

ROLE(S): None

TIME: 20-40 minutes

MATERIALS: A short article from the morning newspaper.

It is necessary to select a space within, or near, the classroom where students can talk softly, yet not be heard by other members of the class. This spot is known as the "safe" area out of earshot of the other students in the class.

The teacher takes one student to the "safe" area and reads the news article to her/him. The teacher leaves the "safe" area, taking the news article with her/him, and directs another student to go to the "safe" area.

The first student repeats the news story to the second student, then leaves the area. A third student is then selected by the teacher to go to the "safe" area where student #2 repeats the story to him/her. This process is continued until each student in class has the opportunity to hear the news story and tell it to another student.

The last student hearing the story returns to the room and tells the story to the entire class.

The teacher then reads the "real" article to the class. In most instances the story told by the last news reporter will vary greatly from the original text.

The teacher then leads a class discussion on the importance of effective speaking and listening skills.

VARIATION: Any reading material, including academic content appropriate for the age group, may be used in this activity. It is important, however, that the material is no longer than one page in length and is complete in and of itself.

— — —

COMBINED SPEAKING AND LISTENING:

THE UNKNOWN DESIGN

GRADE LEVEL: Kindergarten-Adult

ROLE(S): None

TIME: 15-20 minutes

MATERIALS: A geometric design drawn by the teacher, paper, pencils.

The design is placed out of the visual range of the class, such as the backside of a portable chalkboard or behind a room divider.

One student is selected to be the "director." She/he verbally instructs the class to individually reproduce the given design on the paper provided to them.

The students ("artists") may not ask the "director" any questions.

After the "director" has completed giving directions he/she shows the design to the "artists", they then compare their drawings with the original design. A discussion related to the experience is conducted; e.g., "What did the 'director' say that helped you reproduce the design?" "Why were some artists successful in design reproduction and others not?"

VARIATION: This activity may be conducted in pairs, one person being the "director", the other the "artist".

— — —

NONVERBAL LANGUAGE:

FIND THE FEELING

GRADE LEVEL: Kindergarten-Adult

ROLE(S): None

TIME: 10-15 minutes

MATERIALS: Anything displaying pictures of people (e.g. magazines, newspapers).

In small groups of 2 or 3, students are instructed to find all the pictures reflecting a specific feeling (e.g., happy, worried, confused, sad, interested, etc.)

VARIATION: Each student completes assignment individually.

— — —

IDENTIFY THE FEELING

GRADE LEVEL: Kindergarten-Adult

ROLE(S): None

TIME: 5-10 minutes

MATERIALS: Pictures of people

In small groups of 2 or 3, students are given two pictures of people exhibiting different emotions/feelings and are asked to identify what feeling the people are exhibiting.

VARIATION: Use cartoon or "smiley" faces for primary age children.

— — —

MIRRORING

GRADE LEVEL: Kindergarten-Adult

ROLE(S): None

TIME: 6-8 minutes

MATERIALS: None

Students choose partners and stand facing each other. One partner is designated the leader, the other is the "mirror". The leader makes a series of movements, which are followed as closely as possible by the "mirror". After 2-3 minutes the roles are reversed.

CAUTION: Students should be directed to begin with slow movements to give the "mirrors" a fair chance to imitate with ease.

VARIATION: When first beginning this activity, it may be adviseable for teachers of kindergarten and early elementary to be the leader, with the entire class acting as "mirrors".

— — —

MUSIC IS MY BUSINESS

GRADE LEVEL: Preschool-Adult

ROLE(S): None

MATERIALS: Pre-recorded record or tape with appropriate machine.

PRESCHOOL-ADULT

TIME: 5-10 minutes

The music is played to the class. The teacher and students discuss the "way the music makes me feel." The selection is again played for the class and students dance about the classroom reflecting the way the music makes them feel.

GRADE 3-ADULT

TIME: 15-30 minutes

Groups of three or four students are formed. They are instructed to listen to the musical selection (suggested length: 2-3 minutes) and, as a group, develop a nonverbal interpretation of the music. The group product should be limited to 2-3 minutes and may be performed with the music as a direct interpretation or without the music as an indirect interpretation. The groups will perform for the class at the close of the planning period. The interpretation may take the form of a dance, pantomimed skit or any variation thereof. During the planning period (5-15 minutes is suggested) the musical selection should be played softly in the background.

— — —

EXPRESSION!

GRADE LEVEL: Grade 3-Adult

ROLE(S): None

TIME: 20-45 minutes

MATERIALS: 4x6 index cards with one word describing an emotion written on each card (e.g., happy, sad, disgusted, worried, confused, pleased, etc.)

A specific emotion is written on each index card. It is recommended that a minimum of 15 different emotions be represented to add variety to the exercise. The teacher places the cards on the table face down. Each student takes a turn drawing a card, thereby becoming the "actor". The actor shows the card to no one. She/he "acts out" the emotion. The class members attempt to guess which emotion is being demonstrated. It is recommended that a time limit of 2-3 minutes be given each actor. At the end of the time period, or upon a successful guess, the emotion card is shown to the rest of the class.

After each turn the card is placed at the bottom of the stack and the process is repeated with the next student.

— — —

NONVERBAL LANGUAGE ACTIVITIES:

TANGRAMS

GRADE LEVEL: Grade 2-Adult

ROLE(S): Optional: Observer, used in the Variation

TIME: 20 minutes

MATERIALS: Tangram packets for each group of students consisting of four separate tangrams. The tangrams are unmarked and the parts are mixed up within the packets.

Students are divided into groups of 2-5, depending on grade level. Each group is given a packet containing 4 mixed-up tangrams. Group members may not talk with each other or participate in gestural communication. The only communication allowed during this activity is actual movement of the tangram pieces on the table or workspace. Students communicate by giving tangram pieces to each other or helping another student 'try out' a piece he/she thinks might fit.

The student receiving the packet in each group distributes the tangram pieces among the group members. This is done by passing out pieces one at a time, in a clockwise fashion until all pieces have been distributed. (Note: All group members may not have the same number of tangram parts after distribution.)

The group then begins the task of putting the four tangrams together. The guidelines for this activity are: 1) no speaking; 2) no gesturing; 3) pieces may be traded and moved, as desired.

Sample tangrams to be used in this activity are found in Figure 22.

VARIATION: For grades 5-adult, the group role of Observer may be infused into this activity. An observer would be selected for each group. During the process of assembling the tangram pieces, the observer would sit just outside the group and note its directions were being followed and, also, what process was used by group members to achieve success.

— — —

Figure 22: SAMPLE TANGRAMS

Tangrams

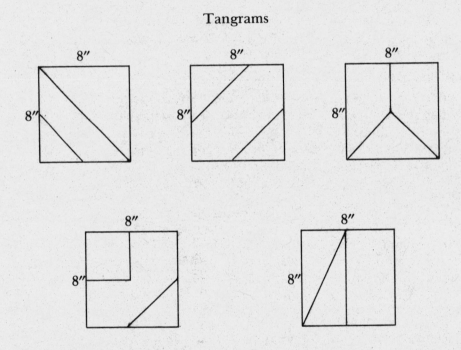

The above patterns are drawn and cut out of 8″ squares. Tangram pieces are "mixed up" and placed in one packet. The facilitator of each group opens the packet and distributes the pieces, one at a time, to group members in the same manner as dealing cards.

PERCEPTION CHECKING NONVERBAL LANGUAGE:
BECOMING AWARE OF YOUR NONVERBAL MESSAGES

GRADE LEVEL: Grade 6-Adult

ROLE(S): None

TIME: 10-15 minutes

MATERIALS: None

In pairs, students tell each other how they "know" the other one is happy, embarrassed, angry, or whatever feeling(s) the teacher specifies.

The receiver/listener can affirm or deny that is what she/he is actually feeling when she/he demonstrates that nonverbal action.

Follow the activity with a class discussion regarding how we can misinterpret others' nonverbal messages and the importance of checking out our perceptions.

SOURCES

EXPERIENCING INATTENTIVENESS/ATTENTIVESS: Peggy

THE ROTTEN CHICKEN: Adapted from THE ROTTEN CHICKEN by Leticia Solomen

LEARNING TO ASK QUESTIONS: Peggy

PARAPHRASING: Peggy

ON BECOMING AN ACTOR: Marvin Roupe, Teacher — Point Arena, CA.

ON BECOMING A POET: Ann Marie Samson, Teacher and Poet — Willits, CA.

NEWS REPORTER: Adapted for Simple Cooperation by Jacquie and Peggy from the "old" telephone game. Original source unknown.

THE UNKNOWN DESIGN: Original source unknown.

FIND THE FEELING: Peggy

IDENTIFY THE FEELING: Peggy

MIRRORING: Original source unknown.

MUSIC IS BY BUSINESS: Original source unknown.

EXPRESSION: Marvin Roupe, Teacher — Point Arena, CA.

TANGRAMS: Both Peggy and Jacquie have experienced this activity many times when attending workshops. Original source unknown.

BECOMING AWARE OF NONVERBAL LANGUAGE: Peggy

CHAPTER 11

BRAINSTORMING

BRAINSTORMING:
PRACTICE TO LEARN CONCEPTS #1

GRADE LEVEL: Grade 4-Adult

ROLE(S): Facilitator and Recorder

TIME: 15-20 minutes

MATERIALS: Felt tip water color marking pen

Group Size: According to grade level, 2-6

Teacher tells the class the following story.

The company has 1 million felt tip marking pens and they don't know what to do with them — they forgot to put the ink in the pens. They do not want to throw them away because they will lose thousands of dollars. We have to think of how we can use these no-ink pens.

Groups of 2-6 students are formed. A facilitator and a recorder are chosen in each group.

Each group brainstorms as many uses for the pens within the time limit of 4 minutes. The teacher acts as the time-keeper. Remember to give students "thinking" time before the brainstorming activity.

At the end of the brainstorming session each facilitator shares his/her group's ideas.

Note: Ideas generated from various groups have included such things as: baby's toy, sell them as invisible ink pens, mobiles, new kind of toy boat or missile, and take the felt out and use as tooth pick holders.

— — —

BRAINSTORMING:

PRACTICE TO UNDERSTAND CONCEPTS #2

GRADE LEVEL: Grade 4-Adult

ROLE(S): Facilitator and Recorder

TIME: 10-15 minutes

MATERIALS: Chart paper and marking pens.

Using almost anything found in a classroom, generate ideas on how it can be used aside from its general use.

Examples:

— chalk board eraser

— pencil eraser

— chalk

— pencils

— record disk

— computer disk

— rulers

After the brainstorming session, the ideas of each group are shared with the class as a whole.

SOURCES:

PRACTICE TO LEARN CONCEPTS #1: Experienced by Peggy in various leadership workshops. Original source unknown.

PRACTICE TO UNDERSTAND CONCEPTS #2: Peggy

CHAPTER 12
BREAKING UP

COMMENTS:

Breaking up activities assist students in bringing closure to the school year. The message that we give students is that we have done something important this school year. We have made new friends, strengthened old relationships, and have added many new academic skills that will stay with us for the rest of our lives.

The activities listed will help immortalize the group and refocus/redirect energy.

- **SHARING INDIVIDUAL PICTURES**
  Bulletin board of individual student pictures — students may bring photos to class or instant camera prints may be used.

- **SHARING CLASS PICTURES**
  A picture of the entire class may be taken, reproduced, and distributed to the students.

- **COPIES OF SPECIAL SMALL GROUP PROJECTS**
  Cooperative groups may wish to reproduce a project that is special to the group to keep as a momento.

- **AUTOGRAPH BOOKS**

- **JOURNALS OR SCRAPBOOKS**
  Group may, as their final project, write a journal or make a scrapbook, noting special events and memories.

- **A CLASS STORY MAY BE WRITTEN AND DUPLICATED FOR EACH MEMBER**

- **SHARING FEELINGS ABOUT WHAT THIS YEAR HAS MEANT AND HOW MUCH WAS ACHIEVED**
  This may be done in small groups, with each group writing their thoughts and feelings and sharing with the class as a whole. Another alternative is to have individuals share in whole class discussion or by conducting a Whip.

- **VISITING THE CLASSROOMS OR SCHOOL THAT THE STUDENTS WILL BE ENROLLED IN THE FOLLOWING YEAR**

- SHARING FUTURE GOALS OR SUMMER ACTIVITIES

- ORIENTATION SESSIONS WITH THE NEXT HIGHER GRADE LEVEL TEACHERS

- PLANTING TREES OR OTHER PLANTS ON THE CAM— PUS GROUNDS AS A PERMANENT MEMORY OF THE GROUP

- PAINTING A MURAL FOR THE CLASSROOM OR SCHOOL AS A PERMANENT MEMORY

  Other art projects such as sculptures may also be used for this purpose.

- GIVING IMAGINARY GIFTS

  Students draw names of other class members and design in their minds, an imaginary gift to give the other person. The class then sits in a large circle and each student shares the gift with the other student. This is done by describing the gift and walking over to the student and placing the imaginary gift in his/her hands.

- LEAVING A GIFT TO THE WORLD

  The class, or small groups, decides on an imaginary gift that, if it were possible, they would give the world. Responses received in the past include clear communication, peace, food for everyone, etc.

SOURCES

We have each used these activities for so many years that we honestly do not know if one or both of us or someone else is the originator of any of them.

APPENDIX

AUTHORS' NOTE:

These next pages describe a cooperative testing activity at the Community College level. It was developed and implemented by Judith Hummer who attended one of our workshops. We have printed the text in Ms. Hummer's own words and with her permission.

We believe this is an excellent example of the steps involved in preparing and conducting a Simple Cooperation activity as well as the results that may be achieved. Judith's final comments reflect the satisfaction that both she and her students experienced.

Finally, as Judith points out, this activity may easily be adapted for use with younger students.

USE OF COOPERATIVE LEARNING: TESTING SKILLS LEARNED
SUBJECT AREA: COMPUTERS

COURSE OBJECTIVE: Students will have a working knowledge of word processing software. (One fourth of the class — Introduction to Microcomputers.)
CLASS SCHEDULE: Meets weekly, 4 hours
STUDENTS: Working adults who attend school in their 'spare' time. (Note: this test could easily be adapted for younger students.)
SCHOOL: Community College
PROBLEMS ENCOUNTERED:

- 2-3 students for each computer;
- only one seat at each computer terminal;
- classroom is separate from lab;
- computer labs are very small;
  - — Lab #1 has 14 computers with 4 printers;
  - — Lab #2 has 8 computers and 2 printers;
- tremendous age range (18-70+ years).

WORK COMPLETED BEFORE TEST:
Lecture and lab on Bank Street Writer (a word processor). Homework that required the student to demonstrate all the capabilities of the word processor as well as his/her ability to manipulate the computer.
PURPOSE OF TEST:

- To observe each student's ability with the computer;

• To observe use of the word processing program;

• To encourage students to work together to solve problems (to teach and learn from each other). Side effect: they get to know other students in the class;

• To demonstrate a more 'natural' working environment with the computer. (Rather than the usually quiet lab with lots of help available from aides);

• To demonstrate how the word processor is normally used. (The homework tends to keep the student within the confined limits of writing: "do this; do that; now move over here..." It's stilted and contrived. This test gives students a chance to see how the word processor can be used such as creative writing at the terminal where every word is not set in concrete.); and

• For grading purposes.

TEST: A writing project.

TIME LIMIT: 3-4 hours

INSTRUCTIONS GIVEN TO CLASS:

WEEK BEFORE TEST:
Remind students that there will be a test the following week. It will be a cooperative, open book test.

"Finish your homework and make sure that you know how to use the word processor. In addition, do the following four things: (write these on the chalk board)

1. Bring a hat;

2. Dress like a writer;

3. Decide what kind of writer you are;

4. Choose a pseudonym (alias)."

At this point, your students will be beside themselves asking questions. Repeat what you've already said. Tell them it will be fun. Smile a lot. Don't tell them any more.

TEST WEEK:
Arrive dressed like "a writer" — whatever that means to you. Be thoughtful about how you dress.

Your students will take their clues from you at the beginning of this exercise. If you dress too conservatively it will set the wrong tone. If you dress relaxed, your students will relax. Remember: they are nervous — you have all the information and they don't know what's going on.

Take the time to look at how everyone is dressed and let them know you noticed. Comment upon it — "It's good to see such a distinguished group of writers." Everyone will probably begin to relax at this point.

EXPLAIN THE PROJECT:

The class project is up to you, the teacher. The assignment should be something that all class members are comfortable with. If there is any doubt in your mind about the student comfort level, pick something else.

The project should be a creative writing assignment in which each class member is responsible for writing a specific part. When put together, all the parts form the whole product.

EXAMPLE #1:

WRITING A BOOK. Each student writes a 'chapter.' 'Chapters' range in length from a couple of paragraphs to over a page. Remember that length depends as much on a student's typing ability as it does on their ability to manipulate the computer and word processor. Also, there are time constraints. Each student will have a limited amount of time to work on the computer.

EXAMPLE #2:

A SERIES OF LETTERS WRITTEN TO 'DEAR ABBY' spanning a character's lifetime. Each letter is dated so that they can be printed in order.

EXAMPLE #3:

WRITING A DIARY for a character. Each entry is dated.

EXAMPLE #4:

WRITING A SERIES OF LIES told by a member of the Liar's Club. Written on April Fool's Day year after year.

Notice that each of these projects requires a single character to be the focal point. That makes the class assignment easier, and creates continuity between all individual student's work.

EXPLAIN THE TESTING PROCEDURE: "This is a Cooperative test. You are all in it together and need each other to complete the task."

Tell them that they do not have to be good writers. Emphasize this. "Your writing ability is not important. I am not testing your writing skills. I am testing your word processing ability and your ease of computer use." Explain that in a project such as this one, bad writing may be better suited; when the parts are put together it makes the book or story more interesting. This is true every time.

The story can be allowed to digress and ramble, passing from one topic to another. It can be a collection of vignettes or sketches. What ties it together is the character that is developed.

CHARACTER DEVELOPMENT:

Character development is the first cooperative part of this test. The first step is to decide on the character's age and sex. Then, divide the class into groups, each of which develops certain aspects of the character's life. OR you can have the entire class brainstorm this together.

Next, describe the group process:

— use consensus decision making (define consensus: what everyone can LIVE with);

— everyone gives input;

— everyone listens to everyone;

— one person in the group lists (records) the information; another (facilitator) checks for consensus;

— 15 minutes for the task.

GROUP ASSIGNMENT:

Group #1: Physical description of character; habits and unusual aspects of character's personality and lifestyle.

Group #2: Occupation and hobbies; major events in character's life (at different ages).

Group #3: Family & friends — central cast of characters.

Group #4: Where character has lived and at what ages; where he/she lives now; schools attended; organizations character belongs to; where he/she goes on vacation.

At the end of the 15 minutes bring the class back together and have each group's recorder write their character information on the chalkboard.

The class should then decide, as a group, on the character's name. Write ALL suggestions on the board — don't be selective. Let the class decide.

Next, decide on the book's title, or page headings.

Now you are ready for the test itself.

THE TEST:

(Before class you should have divided the amount of lab time available by the number of students taking the test.)

Tell the class the maximum number of minutes available for each student to work individually on the computer. Emphasize that this is the MAXIMUM amount of time and that they must time themselves. "This project MUST be completed by the end of class." No extensions of time are allowable. (In doing this project, the mood established in one marathon session is important. It would be impossible to recreate it at a later time.)

Ask that those students who are quick thinkers take a computer first — this will get things rolling. There are always more students ready to begin immediately than there are available computer terminals. This is good. If, however, students seem shy about taking terminals, remind them that by volunteering early they can avoid the crush later.

Inform the students that everyone will stay in class until the project is completed. Be firm about this and you won't have any problems. Otherwise, a few 'worker' students will stay until the very end finishing the 'put-together' work for the entire class, while the others go home. The group will not be a cohesive unit if this happens. Also, there will be a few students who are slow; they should not be left all alone and made to feel incompetent. Early finishers should be encouraged to help others and oversee the completion of the project. Later on in the evening, one terminal could be set aside for games.

Each student's work is to be transferred to the teacher's disk. Saving a file to a different disk is a new experience for them. When they transfer their completed files to the teacher's disk they need to sign a sheet that stays with the disk. The sheet should identify the student's name, date of writing (so that they can be put in order), and the name of the file. Students should check with each other to be sure there are no duplicate file names.

In addition, students should print out their part on a single sheet, write her/his real name on it, and turn it in to you, the teacher. This, along with the index to the disk will be your record of who wrote what.

Students DO NOT sign their writing with their own names. They sign it with their pseudonyms. This is to protect some students from embarassment when the entire class project is printed out and read by all.

Let students know that, as teacher, you will observe, but will not help in any way (except to intervene if there is a cooperation problem). Each student writes and edits her/his own part. They may use their notes on operating the word processor, or another student may help. However, another student may help by giving ONLY verbal instructions — the helping student may not touch the keyboard; the helper must also explain the 'why' of what to do.

If you have a student who really does not want to do creative writing, or who is very restless make him/her the editor. She/he then becomes responsible for creating a title page, table of contents, and overseeing the merging of the stories.

At this point, just step back and allow your students to work. Although they must write about the character, they may pick any aspect or time in his/her life (including events not written on the board).

Toward the end of the class time, when a majority of students have completed their section, temporarily stop the test and give a demonstration on chaining files together for print-out (with continuous page numbers, format, and headings). Then leave them alone, allowing the last ones to finish writing their part and those who are done to print out the project. Since each individual file needs to be chained, this will take a while.

THE RESULT:

You will have:

1. A printed sheet from each student containing the section he/she wrote, with his/her real name written on it.

2. A disk containing each student's file, along with a companion sheet that lists file names, date of file, and student's correct name.

3. A print-out from the entire class of the entire project. It should be numbered correctly, with page headings, and continuous formatting.

NOTE: If you have a smaller class, or are concerned that students will not have enough to do, you can give a 5 minutes hands-on test to each individual student while the main project is going on. Just take over one terminal and have the students come to you individually to do the exercise.

COMMENTS:

This test works because of the way it is set up. If you asked a group of adults if they'd like to go to a costume party and write a book, most of them would say no, even if they were intrigued by the idea. But the smiles and jokes and incredible story lines that have been created when this test has been given attest to its success.

A major part of the success is because the test is cooperative. Everyone is in the same boat, so they decide to paddle. The tone of the test is set in the first 15 minutes. If the teacher is relaxed, the students are relaxed. If the teacher explains clearly that writing style or skills will not be graded, amazing things will be written. People who believe that they can't write at all suddenly begin writing fabulous stuff.

The costuming and the uncertainty before the test begins to add to the atmosphere.

Dressing differently puts students off-guard. They become more creative because they are "not themselves." Students are curious about what will happen and can hardly wait to see what others have written.

Seeing all the parts printed out in one final product is very exciting. There is magic in creation under pressure. The time limit forces decisions to be made about what will be written. Perfectionism is impossible which makes it more realistic.

A lab aide once paid my class what I considered to be the highest compliment, "Your students have gone past the mechanics of using the word processor." By concentrating on the creativity of the project, HOW to do it becomes less important than WHY to do it.

Observing your students during the test provides an extremely accurate picture of how they are doing. It's easy to see if anyone is having problems.

Finally, the students learn two new tricks DURING the test: how to transfer a file to a different disk; and how to chain files together. There's no reason why a test can't be an opportunity to learn.

Most of all, everyone has FUN. There are lots of smiles.

GLOSSARY

AUTOCRATIC DECISION: One person unilaterally makes decision for all.

BEHAVIOR: An action that is tangible, quantifible.

BRAINSTORMING: Generating ideas, without evaluation, usually allowing very short periods of time (3-7 minutes).

CHECKER: Compares accuracy of group's answers with the answer key; especially valuable for math, spelling and other activities where there is a single, correct answer.

CHECKING-OUT PERCEPTIONS: Asking speaker if what you think the speaker is feeling/saying is accurate.

CONGRUENCE: Verbal and nonverbal messages are saying the same thing.

CONSENSUS DECISION: Group as a whole makes decision — final decision may not be each individual's favorite, but all agree they can "live-with" and support the decision.

DEMOCRATIC DECISION: Involves some type of voting.

EFFECTIVE COMMUNICATION: Transference of ideas, thoughts, attitudes and opinions from a sender (speaker), to a receiver (listener), with the receiver understanding the message in the same manner that the sender intended.

ENERGIZING ACTIVITIES: Brief activities to assist students regain energy — usually an activity which is very different than the present task; intended to "cure" glazed eyes, inability to attend to the task, etc.

FACILITATOR:

AS MONITOR — Similar to "old" monitor role — gets and distributes papers and other resources group needs, turns group work in to teacher.

STUDENT — Helps group fulfill its objective; concerned more with group process than with group product.

TEACHER — Assists students with the process of information gathering, decision making and problem solving.

GETTING ACQUAINTED ACTIVITIES: Short activities designed to help students know each other and the teacher.

INTERNAL DIALOGUE: Talking to ourselves within our mind.

NONVERBAL MESSAGE: All parts of message except spoken words; includes tone, tempo, volume, eye movement, facial expression, gestures, etc.

OBSERVER: Using observation form does frequency count of specific behavior(s) which have been previously identified by teacher, of each group member or group as a whole; reports back to group quantitatively, without evaluation.

PARAPHRASING: Saying, in your own words, your understanding of the speaker's message.

PARTICIPATORY DECISION: Input/suggestions are given to decision maker who considers the input when making decision.

PRAISER: During specific time periods identified by the teacher, provides praise and compliments to group members for doing certain behavior(s) (specified by the teacher).

RECORDER:

> **BEGINNING/SINGLE ASSIGNMENT** — Writes group's answers to give to teacher.

> **ADVANCED/PROBLEM SOLVING AND BRAINSTORMING** — Writes key elements of group discussion and its decisions.

SIMPLE COOPERATION: Method of integrating social and academic skills within homogeneous or heterogeneous student groups.

STANDARDS: Classroom behavioral norms and values; sets a framework of expectations.

TIME-KEEPER: Keeps track of how much time the group has used and how much is left to complete the assignment.

TRANSITION ACTIVITIES: Brief activities to ease of movement from one lesson to another; an activity to refocus individual student's energy from him/herself and what he/she was doing to the group task — especially useful after lunch, breaks, recess, and at the beginning of secondary school class periods.

WRAP-UP: Brief activity at the end of each Simple Cooperation lesson which brings closure to the lesson, integrates thinking and communication skills, and gives teacher feedback regarding student learning; related to thinking skills and academic or social objective. Teacher may use this feedback to adjust and monitor lessons.

REFERENCES

Ackoff, Russel; The Art of Problem Solving. New York: John Wiley and Sons, 1978.

Aronson, E. and N. Blaney, C. Stephan, J. Sikes, M. Snapp; The Jigsaw Classroom. Beverly Hills, CA: Sage Publications, 1978.

Canfield, Jack and Harold C. Wells; 100 Ways to Enhance Self-Concept in the Classroom. Englewood Cliffs, N.J.: Prentice Hall, 1976.

Cathcart, Robert S.; Small Group Communication. Dubuque Iowa: Wm. C. Brown Company Publishers, 1979.

Center for Multisensory Learning, University of California Berkley, SAVI/SELPH. Lawrence Hall of Science, 1976. (Note: this is a science program, based on small group instruction, lesson plans are included.)

Cetron, Marvin; Schools of the Future. New York: McGraw Hill, 1985

Co-operative College of Canada; Co-operation and Community Life, 1983. Order from: Co-operative College of Canada, 141-105 Street West, Saskatoon, Saskatchewan S7N 1N3.

Co-operative College of Canada; Co-Operative Outlooks, 1983. Order from Co-operative College of Canada.

Doyle, Michael and David Straus; How to Make Meetings Work. New York: Playboy Paperbacks, 1976.

Educators for Social Responsibility, Perspectives. Cambridge Mass: Educators for Social Responsibility, 1983.

Feingold, Norman S. and Norma Reno Miller; Emerging Careers: New Occupations for the Year 2000 and Beyond. Maryland: Garrett Park Press.

Feingold, Norman S.; "Emerging Careers, Occupations for Post-Industrial Society," The Futurist. 9-16 (Feb. 1984).

Feuerstein, Reuven; The Dynamic Assessment of Retarded Performers. Baltimore, Md.: University Park Press, 1979.

Feuerstein, Reuven; Instrumental Enrichment. Baltimore, MD: University Park Press, 1980.

Gibbs, Jeanne and Andre Allen; Tribes: A Process For Peer Involvement. CA: Center for Human Development, 1978.

Gordon, Dr. Thomas; Leader Effectiveness Training. Wynden Books, 1977.

Gordon, Dr. Thomas; Parent Effectiveness Training in Action. New York: G.P. Putnam and Sons, 1976.

Grinder, John and Richard Bandler; The Structure of Magic II. Santa Clara, CA: Science and Behavior Books Inc., 1976.

Harris M.D., Thomas A.; I'm OK—Your OK. New York: Avon Books, 1969.

Johnson, David W.; Reaching Out. Englewood Cliffs, N.J.: Prentice Hall, 1981.

Johnson, David and Frank Johnson; Joining Together. Englewood Cliffs, N.J., Prentice Hall, 1982.

Johnson, David and Roger T. Johnson; Learning Together and Alone, Cooperation, Competition and Individualization. Englewood Cliffs, N.J.: Prentice Hall, 1975.

Johnson, David and Roger T. Johnson, Edythe Johnson Holuber, Patricia Roy; Circles of Learning. ASC Publications, 1984.

Judson, Stephanie; A Manual on Nonviolence and Children. Order from: Nonviolence and Children Program, Friends Peace Committee, 1515 Cherry Street, Philadelphia, Penn. 19102.

Kaplan, Phyllis G. and Susan K. Crawford, Shelley L. Nelson; Nice Nifty Innovations for Creative Expression. Denver, Colorado: Love Publishing Company, 1977.

Kagan, Spencer; Cooperative Learning Resources for Teachers, 1985. Order from: Professor Spencer Kagan, School of Education, University of California, Riverside, CA 92521.

Kaufman, Roger; Identifying and Solving Problems: A System Approach. San Diego, CA: University Associates, Inc. 1979.

McCabe Ed.D., Margaret E.; The Public High School in the Year 2010: A National Delphi Study. Unpublished Dissertation, University of LaVerne: LaVerne CA.

Meichenbaum, Donald; Cognitive Behavior Modification. New York: Plenum Press, 1979.

Moorman, Chick and Dee Dishon; Our Classroom: We Can Learn Together. Michigan: The Institute for Personal Power, 1983.

Moskowitz, Gertrude; Caring and Sharing in the Foreign Language Class. Rowley Mass: Newbury House Publishers, 1978.

Naisbitt, John; Megatrends. New York: Warner Books, 1982.

New Games Foundation, Andrew Fluegelman ed.; The New Games Book. Doubleday.

Nierenberg, Gerard and Henry H. Calero; Meta Talk. New York: Pocket Books, 1975.

Orcutt Union School District, Project Class. 1981/82. Order from: Orcutt Union School District, P.O. Box 2310, Orcutt, CA 93455.

Poirier, Gerard; Students as Partners in Team Learning. Berkeley, CA: Center of Team Learning, 1970.

Prutzman, Priscilla and M. Leonard; The Friendly Classroom For a Small Planet, 1978. Order from Children's Creative Response to Conflict, 15 Rutherford Place, New York, New York 10003.

Reid, Jo-Anne and Peter Forrestal, Jonathon Cook; Small Group Work In The Classroom, 1982. Order from: The Manager, Education Supplies Branch, 23 Miles Road, Kewdale 6105, Western Australia.

Saskatchewan Department of Co-Operation and Co-operative Development; Working Together, Learning Together, 1983. Order from: The Steward Resource Centre, S.T.F., Box 1108, Saskatoon, Saskatchewan S7K 3N3.

Schmuck, Richard and Patricia Schmuck; A Humanistic Psychology of Education. Making the School Everybody's House. Palo Alto, CA: Mayfield Publishing Co., 1974.

Schmuck, R. and P. Schmuck; Group Process in the Classroom, Fourth Edition, Wm. C. Brown Co., 1983.

Schniedwind, Nancy and Ellen Davidson; Open Minds to Equity: A sourcebook of Learning Activities To Promote Race, Sex, Class and Age Equity. New Jersey: Prentice Hall, 1983.

Sharan, Shlomo and Yael Sharan; Small-Group Teaching. New Jersey: Educational Technology Publications, 1976.

Sharan, Shlomo and Paul Hare, D. Clark, Rachel Hertz-Lazarowitz; Cooperation in Education. Utah: Brigham Young University Press.

Slavin, Robert E.; Cooperative Learning: Student Teams. Washington D.C.: National Education Association, 1982.

Slavin, Robert E.; Cooperative Learning. New York: Longman, 1983.

Slavin, Robert E.; Using Student Team Learning, The Johns Hopkins Team Learning Project. Baltimore, MD: Johns Hopkins University, 1980.

Solomon, Letitia Ursa; The Rotten Chicken. Ukiah, CA: Henchanted Books, Box 804, Ukiah, CA 95482. 1984.

Stanford, G.; Developing Effective Classroom Groups: A Practical Guide for Teachers. Canada: Hart Publishing Co. LTD., 1977. (Out of print.)

Stein, Sherman and Calvin D. Crabill; Elementary Algebra. A Guided Inquiry. Mass.: Houghton Mifflin, 1972.

Vacha, Edward and William McDonald, Joan Coburn, Harold Black; Improving Classroom Social Climate: Teacher's Handbook. New York: Holt, Rinehart & Winston, 1979.

Whimbey, Arthur and Linda Shaw Whimbey; Intelligence Can Be Taught: New York: Bantam Books, 1976.

INDEX

Please use this form to order additional copies.
All orders must be prepaid.

QUAN.	ISBN 0-933935-07-2	PRICE	TOTAL
	Simple Cooperation in the Classroom	$15.95	
Shipping and Handling FOR EACH BOOK ORDERED: Within Continental USA — add $1.50 Outside Continental USA — add $2.50			
	SUB-TOTAL		
California only — add .96 Sales Tax per book			
	TOTAL		

SHIP TO:

_____

_____

_____

_____

MAIL CHECK OR MONEY ORDER & ORDER FORM TO:
ITA PUBLICATIONS
P.O. BOX 1599
WILLITS, CA 95490

For quantity prices, over 100 copies call: (707) 459-6100

Thank you.